D0400724

PIMLICO

328

THE LAST COWBOY

Jane Kramer has been a writer on the staff of the *New Yorker* since 1964. She is the author of numerous books, including *Unsettling Europe* and *Europeans*.

THE LAST
COWBOY

JANE KRAMER

PIMLICO

Published by Pimlico 1998

2 4 6 8 10 9 7 5 3 1

© Jane Kramer 1977

This book is sold subject to the condition that it shall not,
by way of trade or otherwise, be lent, resold, hired out, or otherwise
circulated without the publisher's prior consent in any form of binding
or cover other than that in which it is published and without a
similar condition including this condition being imposed
on the subsequent purchaser

This work was originally published in the *New Yorker*

First published in the United States of America by
Harper and Row, Publishers, Inc., 1977
Pimlico edition 1998

Pimlico
Random House
20 Vauxhall Bridge Road,
London SW1V 2SA

Random House Australia (Pty) Limited
20 Alfred Street, Milsons Point, Sydney,
New South Wales 2061, Australia

Random House New Zealand Limited
18 Poland Road, Glenfield, Auckland 10, New Zealand

Random House South Africa (Pty) Limited
Endulini, 5A Jubilee Road, Parktown 2193, South Africa

Random House UK Ltd Reg. No. 954009

A CIP catalogue record for this book is available from the Britixh Library

ISBN 0-7126-6614-1

Papers used by Random House UK Limited are natural,
recyclable products made from wood grown in sustainable forests.
The manufacturing processes conform to the environmental
regulations of the country of origin

Printed and bound in Great Britain
by Mackays of Chatham PLC

For my daughter, Wicky,
who came to Texas with me

The Last Cowboy

Chapter 1

Henry Blanton turned forty on an April day when the first warm winds of spring crossed the Texas Panhandle and the diamondback rattlers, fresh and venomous from their winter sleep, came slipping out from under the cap rock of the Canadian River breaks. It was a day full of treachery and promise, the kind of day that Henry would have expected for the showdown in a good Western. Henry was particular about Westerns. When he was a boy and hired out in the summer—for fifty cents a day and the privilege of keeping a local rancher's thirsty cows from ambling downriver from their summer pasture—he saved his pay in a rusty tin bank shaped like a bull and planned a winter's worth of Westerns at Amarillo's movie houses. At night, summers, with the covers pulled tight

1

above his head, Henry braved the moaning ghosts who rode the river breeze past the old stone line camp where he slept alone—and the way he did it was by fixing his thoughts on calm, courageous movie cowboys. He never summoned up the image of his father, who once had been as fine a cowboy as any man in the Panhandle, or the image of his Granddaddy Abel, who had made the long cattle drive to Wyoming back when Indians were still marauding and a rustler with a long rope would as often as not shoot a trail boss who rode out looking for his strays. Henry, deep in his bedroll, shoring up courage against the river's dead, called on John Wayne, Gary Cooper, and Glenn Ford. Especially Glenn Ford. He was convinced then that for "expressin' right," as he put it, there had never been a cowboy to equal Glenn Ford—and he was still convinced of this at forty.

"Expressin' right" was important to the man I call Henry Blanton. It was a gift that he had lost, and he did not know why and was ashamed of himself anyway for wondering, since part of expressing right as a cowboy had to do with the kind of quiet certainty that sustained a man when times were bad. Henry believed that other men might talk to themselves too much, like women, or fret and complain, but a proper cowboy did not. When he watched a Western now, on the big television console he had bought on credit the day the electric lines reached his house on the Willow Ranch, it was less for pleasure or amusement, or even courage, than to find a key to the composure that eluded him. Henry never doubted his abilities as a cowboy. He was the foreman of ninety thousand acres, and he ran them well, considering that he had to take his orders from a rancher who had moved to Eaton Square, in London, and that those orders came to him through a college-boy ranch manager who knew more about juggling account books than raising cattle and was so terrified of cows anyway that he did most of his managing from the driver's seat of a locked, air-conditioned Buick. Henry was a good rider and a fine roper. He could pull a calf with considerable skill, and when he had to he could cut a dogie from the belly of its dying mother. He could account for every one of the twenty-two hundred cows in his charge as if they were his own. He knew which cows delivered strong, healthy calves each spring, which cows needed help calving, which ones tended to miss a year or deliver stillborn. He knew by instinct when a fence was down or a pole had rotted. He could put his ear to the pump pipe of a windmill well that was drawing poorly and tell in minutes whether the checks were broken or the water, three hundred and fifty feet underground, was drying up. He had all those skills, but somehow he was not the sort of cowboy who inspired admiration or respect.

People regarded Henry with exasperation or indulgence. There was something unsettled about his character—something that made him restless and a little out of control. He could not quite manage that economy of gesture and person which was appropriate in a cowboy. Some frustration drove him to a kind of inept excess. He drank too much in town, and worked with a bottle of bourbon in his Ford pickup truck and another bottle in his saddlebag. His stunts were famous—people still talked about the time Henry and his brother, Tom, backed a wild mare into a Pampa funeral parlor—but lately they had turned ugly and immodest. He was hard on his wife, Betsy, and neighbors had begun to

3

remark that he was getting hard on his animals, too. He moved his cows a little too fast for their placidity, drove his yearlings a little too fast for their daily gain. When he worked cattle these days, he was apt to forget to keep his knife sharpened. Sometimes, dehorning, he sawed too deep into a calf's horns, and the creature's lowing turned mad with pain.

Henry had lived on ranches where his camp was thirty or forty miles from a paved road; ranches where Betsy had to cart water from a spring to do the dishes or wash her babies' diapers; ranches where even the best cowboy was worth no more to his boss than a hundred and fifty dollars a month in wages, a shack for a home, and the meat from steers that were too scrawny to send to auction. He did not like to complain about his life now, in a neat prefabricated house with electricity and a telephone and running water —a house with a highway only twelve miles away down a negotiable dirt road. But a rancher could trust his foreman with ninety thousand or nine hundred thousand acres and still regard him as a kind of overgrown boy who was best protected from himself by a stern paternal hand guiding him through a life's indenture.

The movies Henry loved had told him that a good cowboy was a hero. They had told him that a cowboy lived by codes, not rules—codes of calm, solitude, and honor—and that a cowboy had a special arrangement with nature and, with his horse under him and the range spread out around him, knew a truth and a freedom and a satisfaction that ordinary men did not. Even the circuit preacher who came to town every second Sunday claimed that, while no one was really free, a man on a horse surely had a head start in

4

the business of grace over Communists and New Yorkers and all the other sinners who lived by malice and greed. But the movies were changing—they were full of despair lately. The preacher himself had started making money giving I.Q. tests to the Baptists on his route for a rich Bible college that was running a study called God and Intellect. And Henry, turning forty, had little to show for his life as a cowboy except a hand-tooled saddle and a few horses. Betsy had baked a cake, but she was not speaking to him that birthday morning. His daughter Melinda, washing for school, had used up all the hot water. Henry began his forty-first year with a hangover and an icy shower, and, pulling on his boots, he brooded about the future. The West was full of fences and feedyards now. It was crowded with calf traders and futures brokers, college boys who didn't know a Hereford from an Angus, and ranchers who commuted from London or the South of France—and, whatever the movies once promised, there was not much chance, in a showdown, for a hero on a horse.

Chapter 2

T HE first American cowboy was probably a rustler—
one of the men from Stephen Austin's Texas col-
ony who rode south into the Nueces Valley in the
eighteen-twenties and stole longhorns from Mexican ran-
cheros' herds. It took the rest of the century and the imagi-
nation of Easterners to produce a proper cowboy—a cowboy whom children could idolize, and grown men, chafing
at their own domesticated competence, hold as a model of
some profoundly masculine truth. The proper cowboy had
less to do with any Austin colonist than with Owen Wister's
Virginian, riding west onto the vast liminal stage of the
American plains to shoot straight, with a noble and virtu-
ous heart, and kill his villain. The proper cowboy was a
fiction appropriate to a frontier so wild and inhospitable

that most Easterners regarded it as a landscape of Manichaean possibilities. He became for those Easterners the frontier's custodian. They made him Rousseau's Émile with a six-gun. They turned man-in-nature into a myth of natural man, and added natural justice to ease the menace of a place that lay beyond their hegemony and their institutions. They saw to it that he was born good, and that if he died violently, he died wise and defiant and uncorrupted. They set him against outlaws and spoilers, card sharks and Comanches. Their fears became his own sworn enemies. When the myth demanded that they meet—the Virginian paying his duty call on his bride's New England family—he showed them up, with his solemn, masculine behavior, as weak men and petty moralists. And the weak men and petty moralists were reassured.

The West, of course, had other, older heroes. By the cowboy's time, Western folklore was already full of trappers and explorers and pioneering farmers, but they had carried some psychic legacy of the East with them in their canoes and wagons, and the cowboy had not. The trappers who crossed the timberline into the North American wilderness were, in fact, Yankee woodsmen, crowded out of home and pushing west toward a lost privacy that had more to do with Eastern forests than with Western plains. The farmers who followed them were immigrants, mostly, bringing to their homestead claims a romantic European dream of rural life. The historian Henry Nash Smith once said that their vision was the vision of the garden plot. It was a vision refreshed by the prospect of an extraordinarily spacious continent, but it was rooted in Europe just the same. The trouble they had with the cowboys and cattlemen who tried to stop them always involved much more than rights-of-way and fences; it had to do with different notions of what the West meant. The farming settlers of our folklore, rattling across the prairie in Conestoga wagons with their hearty, bonneted wives and broods of children, their chests of pots and pans and quilts, their plows and oxen, shared a republican dream of modest property and the rules and rhythms of domestic law. But the cowboy carried no baggage. Like the frontier, he had no past and no history. He dropped into the country's fantasies mysterious and alone, the way the Virginian arrived one day in his Wyoming town—by right, and not for any reason that he cared to give. With his gun and his horse and his open range, he followed the rules and rhythms of unwritten law and took counsel from his own conscience. He stood for the kind of imperial vision that staked out cattle kingdoms and for the kind of sweeping, solitary power that vigilantes and guardian angels have.

People looked west in the nineteenth century and were inspired to the most jingoistic rhetoric. They talked about manifest destiny and the restless eagle of expansion, and took their images from politicians like the Mississippi Democrat who, eying independent Texas, once demanded, "Who will desire to check the young eagle of America, now refixing her gaze upon our former limits, and repluming her pinions for her returning flight?" Those images suited a people determined to expand across the continent and profit from it. And the cowboy, decked out in his qualities like a knight of their frontier, represented something original and indigenous—something, to their satisfaction, necessarily American. He gave the field of their expansion a

8

kind of mythic geography. They, in turn, gave him extravagant prerogatives, which they later claimed for themselves. A cowboy shook hands where ordinary men signed contracts. A cowboy drew his gun where ordinary men went home. A cowboy took the land for his cattle where ordinary men applied for deeds at the local courthouse. A cowboy claimed the right-of-way where ordinary men built fences and paid tolls.

There was not much room in the cowboy myth for the real cowboys of the nineteenth century—range bums and drifters and failed outlaws, freed slaves and impoverished half-breeds, ruined farmers from the Reconstruction South and the tough, wild boys from all over who were the frontier's dropouts, boys who had no appetite for the ties of land or family, who could make a four-month cattle drive across a thousand miles and not be missed by anyone. But eventually the myth, with its code and its solemn rhetoric, caught up with most of them, and if it left them still outside the law, at least it took the edge off their frightful lawlessness and made a virtue of their old failures. Henry Blanton's grandfather Abel was one of the ruined farmers. The Blantons had lost their five slaves to the Thirteenth Amendment and their Georgia hog farm to carpetbaggers, and Abel, at sixteen, had left for Texas, hired out as a trail hand, and, after ten years in a bedroll, as he liked to say, collected a mail-order bride at the Amarillo depot. It was 1892. Owen Wister's cowboy had settled down to a sober prosperity and was on his way to becoming "an important man, with a strong grip on many various enterprises, and able to give his wife all and more than she asked or desired." And Amarillo was a boom town, with two rail-

9

roads crossing, a drygoods store, and a street of whore-houses. Ranchers around the town had abandoned cattle drives to graze their herds at home in fenced pastures and ship them, fat, by rail to the Illinois and Missouri auctions. Bankers and brokers from London and Edinburgh had bought up Panhandle land, and they were turning cattle kingdoms into cattle companies. The business of running cattle had become big business by the time Abel Blanton brought a bride out to Texas. But there were still ranchers around who paid part of a cowboy's wages in calves or let a favorite hand claim mavericks. Cowboys, with luck, could run a few steers on their ranchers' land along with the ranch cattle, put the profit from those steers toward a couple of sections, and talk about becoming ranchers themselves. Few of them succeeded—only enough to make a man like Henry Blanton bitter that his grandfather had not. The West that Henry mourned belonged to the Western movie, where the land and the cattle went to their proper guardians and brought a fortune in respect and power. It was a West where the best cowboy got to shoot the meanest outlaw, woo the prettiest schoolteacher, bed her briefly to produce sons, and then ignore her for the finer company of other cowboys—a West as sentimental and as brutal as the people who made a virtue of that curious combination of qualities and called it the American experience.

Chapter 3

THE road to Henry Blanton's house began as a narrow, rutted cowpath off a highway north of the town of Canadian, and the only thing that distinguished it from a hundred other cowpaths off that stretch of highway was the big, rusty Willow Ranch brand that swayed, suspended, from an arch above the ranch gate. The brand made a fine target for the high-school boys from town who liked to cruise the highway nights in their fathers' pickups, taking potshots. Henry had to keep a standing order with the local blacksmith for a new brand every other year, but all in all he took the damage philosophically. Everyone he knew owned guns and rifles, and liked to use them. Henry himself carried a .30–30 Winchester slung across the gun rack on his Ford pickup. He believed that hiding weapons was low and cowardly—that a man's right to arm himself against villainy was something sacred, and came straight from God. Lately, of course, there was not much villainy of the sort that Henry and his neighbors could take on with a rifle or a six-gun. They heard a lot about the criminals down in Amarillo, but Amarillo was almost a hundred and fifty miles away, and out in the country people had to content themselves with shooting rattlers and coyotes. The only criminals they were apt to meet were a few fast-talking cattle dealers who specialized in swindling widows and were always safely across the state line anyway by the time people started looking for them.

The land on either side of the Willow gate was flat, irrigated land, planted in wheat for winter grazing, and by April it was almost ready for harvesting. The path ran straight between those precious wheat fields, following a line of wire fence that carried a mean dose of electric current. But once the grassland started, the path began to dip and curve. It followed a fence here, circled a patch of burned-out mesquite there, and veered off toward a windmill somewhere else. The land turned vivid and surprising then. Old, gnarled cactus, tall as trees, sprouted delicate, obscene caps of yellow flowers. Tiny white blossoms sprinkled themselves like spun sugar over the fanning spikes of giant yucca plants. The short blue-grama grass of the pastures, moist and green for a month before the summer sun began to cure it, made strange patches on the clay soil. And cows blocked the path at every turning. They stood motionless in the mud while their calves suckled—stubborn, melancholy creatures, staring out over the scrubby land as if it puzzled and repelled them. For miles, the only sign of human life was an old bunkhouse where Henry's three Mexican hands lived, along with a simple drifter named Jerome, who had wandered onto the ranch a couple of years ago, and who cooked for the Mexicans now and did their wash in exchange for a share of the bunkhouse food, a bed, and the Mexicans' reluctant company. But the road wound on and on, tracing enormous curves across the pastures. Twelve miles in from the highway, it dipped behind a little rise shaded by hackberry trees and cottonwoods, and there it trailed off into a footpath to the Blantons' front door.

Henry's camp was the ranch headquarters. Henry could stand at his door and look across a dirt courtyard to a sheet-metal barn the size of an airplane hangar which held nearly all the supplies he needed to run the Willow. Over the nine years that Henry had worked the ranch, the barn had grown by sections. Just last year, sixty feet had been added, but Henry had seen to it that the things that pleased him most as a cowboy were still within sight of his courtyard. The little hill, with its grove of hackberries and cottonwoods. The shabby, solitary willow by the well. The pasture where his horses grazed. The wooden pens, off the barn, where the milk cows and the dogies fed from troughs, and where Melinda, at fourteen, scrubbed and curried and adored her new roan, Sugar. The old chuck wagon that Abel Blanton once used on roundups—Henry had rescued it for twenty dollars and a promise to haul it home when the Caliche Ranch, where his grandfather had worked for thirty years, was sold to an Eastern conglomerate. By now, all the paraphernalia of modern ranching was well hidden behind the barn, out of sight of the house and the courtyard. Henry

13

worked there when he had to—when he and his hands were branding the little calves that arrived regularly, in truckloads, from farms in Mississippi and Louisiana. Henry had improvised a kind of outdoor assembly line behind the barn. It was a line of ramps and chutes and sprayers ending up at one of the huge iron clamps that cowboys refer to tenderly as "calf cradles" and that can flatten a struggling calf with the turn of a handle and tip it onto its side for the ordeal of castration, branding, and dehorning. The cradle at the Willow was only two years old, but thousands of head of the mangy Southern calves—Mississipps or Okies, the cowboys called them—that Henry's rancher bought and grazed for quick profit had already been run through it. It was foul with a crust of blood and feces which no spring rain could wash away.

Sometimes, toward evening, Betsy climbed onto a rail of one of the rough pine cattle chutes, with her copy of *Woman's Day* and a glass of sweet iced tea, to watch the sunset. There was a fine view west, from the chutes, to the Canadian breaks, and Betsy had always loved that moment just before the sun dropped, when the cliffs lit up like a jagged slash of fire on the horizon. But she could never persuade Henry to sit and watch with her. *His* favorite place for sitting was the driver's seat of his Granddaddy Abel's chuck wagon, which he kept parked under the willow tree. Henry had restored the wagon and was proud of it. The job had taken the better part of three days and nights, with Henry living out of his pickup in a pasture on the Caliche Ranch, but he had been determined. By the time Betsy got worried and sent a state trooper out to find him, he had mended the rotting boards with scraps of barn siding, painted the chuck box, realigned the wheels, and was heading home. The trooper found him easily—driving up the highway with the ancient wagon rattling along behind his pickup and a pint of bourbon in his hand. There was a brief bad moment between them after the trooper suggested taking Henry into town for a breath test. Henry had to explain that he was hauling his granddaddy's chuck wagon home to the family, where it belonged, so that no son-of-a-bitch corporation college boys would ever get the opportunity to pretty it up like a dude-ranch buggy and show it off to their Wall Street friends on hunting-season picnics. Then, of course, the state trooper repented. He even joined Henry in the pickup for some reminiscing. They knew each other well enough for that—they were old antagonists, in the way that cowboys and lawmen were meant to be antagonists, and between them they could count up eight serious confrontations over fights and stunts. But, sitting together in the Ford pickup on the hot, dusty day that Henry brought his grandfather's chuck wagon home, they shared a momentary truce, mourning the West that was supposed to be—mourning, even, their old, useless animosity.

After that, Henry did his best to introduce the chuck wagon to the Willow. Once, for a spring roundup, he fitted the wagon out with pots and pans, a water keg, and bedrolls, and ordered one of his Mexican hands to practice making sourdough biscuits and coleslaw and rhubarb pie from Betsy's "Chuck Wagon Cookbook." He wanted his hands and all the neighbors who would be helping on the roundup to sleep out under the stars, the way cowboys used to do in Abel Blanton's time. And everybody did sleep out

15

—the first night. Henry brought his harmonica, and Tom —who always neighbored for his brother, despite the fact that their ranchers had not spoken since a lawsuit over some gas-drilling rights five years earlier—brought his guitar. The men sang and drank and enjoyed their pie and managed to put away an entire side of spit-roasted grass-fed beef. They had a splendid time, in fact, until the wind blew up and the bugs, attracted by the campfires and the cooking smells, started coming. By morning, they were grumpy and exhausted. And by late afternoon, after roping and branding some three hundred frisky calves, they had all mumbled apologies and were leading their horses to their horse trailers and heading home to hot baths, kitchen dinners, and dry beds. Henry spent that night in a pasture with the woeful Mexican cook, who served him another fine chuck-wagon supper and then went off to eat alone, because Henry did not really approve of breaking bread with wetbacks. Henry still brought the wagon out to roundups, but by now the gesture was more ceremonial than practical, and he always hauled it home after supper. Summers, the local cowboys' children borrowed it for serving hot dogs and Dr Pepper at their Peewee Rodeo, but mostly it stayed put under the willow, where Henry could sit and daydream in the morning while he waited for his hands.

Henry was up at six most spring and summer mornings —in winter, when the days were short, he got up at five— and on school days he helped Melinda with the barn chores, which were hard for her to manage by herself, now that her three older sisters were grown and gone. While Betsy was in the kitchen grilling the bacon and eggs and making coffee, they fed the milk cows and groomed the horses. Sometimes Melinda would lead the horses out to the small pasture off the courtyard. More often lately Henry did it for her, stopping on his way back to breakfast to fill his pickup at the gas tank by the last barn door and to switch off the two-way radio that Lester Hill, the Willow ranch manager, had insisted on installing in the truck a couple of years ago. The radio, set to a base station at Lester's house, shamed Henry. He kept it on when he was touring the ranch alone or doing the chores at headquarters, but when he imagined Lester, mornings, loafing in pajamas by the swimming pool of his fancy new house on the edge of town, the picture convinced him that no ranch manager would ever get the chance to challenge his authority when he was with his hands.

Henry valued his authority. He hurried through break-fast so that he could always greet his men with the day's orders looking relaxed and confident. He liked to sit on the wagon, waiting, with his scratch pad in his hand and a pencil behind his ear, and he made it a point to be properly dressed for the morning's work in his black boots, a pair of clean black jeans, and his old black hat and jacket. Henry liked wearing black. The Virginian, he had heard, wore black, and so had Gary Cooper in the movie "High Noon," and now Henry wore it with a kind of innocent pride, as if the color carried respect and a hero's stern, elegant quali-ties. Once, Betsy discovered him at the bathroom mirror dressed in his black gear, his eyes narrowed and his right hand poised over an imaginary holster. She teased him about it then—at least, until he got so mad that he stayed out half the night in town drinking—but a few weeks later she took a snapshot of him in that same gear and sent it to the Philip Morris company, with a note saying that in her opinion Henry Blanton was much more impressive as a cowboy than the people they used to advertise their Marlboro cigarettes. Henry was, in fact, a handsome man. He was tall and rugged, and ranch life had seasoned the smooth, round face that grinned, embarrassed, in the tinted wedding picture that Betsy kept on the upright piano in her parlor. There was a fine-lined, weathered look about Henry at forty. Too much bourbon and beer had put a gut on him, but his gray eyes were clear and quick most days, and often humorous, and his sandy hair had got thick and wiry as it grayed—a little rumpled and overgrown, because he hated haircuts, though never long enough to cause comment in a cowboy bar. He had a fine, solemn swagger. Saturday nights at the country-and-Western dance in Pampa, he thumped around the floor, serious and sweating, and the women liked to watch him—there was something boyish and charming about his grave self-consciousness. When he was younger, he used to laugh and bow and shake hands with everybody after a good polka. Now, more often than not, he blinked and looked around, suddenly embarrassed, and his laugh was loud and nervous, and made the women who had been watching him uncomfortable.

Betsy attributed the change in Henry to disappointment and drinking. She did not really approve of drinking. She did not want liquor in her house—none of the cowboys' wives she knew did—and even Henry agreed that there was something a little indecent about a bottle of bourbon on display in a Christian living room. Henry drank with guile

18

—the guile of a schoolboy waiting to be caught and punished. It gave an edge to his pleasure, and turned his evasions of the household rules into an artful and immensely satisfying pastime. Besides the bottles in his pickup and his saddlebag, he kept a fifth of Jim Beam hidden behind some old cereal boxes on the top shelf of a kitchen cabinet and another stashed underneath the chuck-wagon seat. He liked to have a drink in the mornings with his white cowhands, but he was careful never to bring the wagon bottle out until his daughter and his wife were gone.

Usually, Melinda left first, careening down the cowpath in an old ranch jeep that Henry had overhauled years earlier to get his daughters to the Willow gate, where the school bus stopped at seven-thirty and, again, late in the afternoon. Then Betsy followed in the family Chevrolet. Betsy worked as an invoice clerk in a grain-sorghum dealer's warehouse thirty miles down the highway. Given the condition of the cowpath and the Panhandle weather, she had to spend some two and a half hours every day commuting, and in spring and summer, with tornado warnings out so often, there were nights when she had to stay in town and sleep at a cousin's house. The drive tired her, and the job had begun to bore her, but she kept working, because the family depended on the money that she made. She liked to say that the ranch took care of everything they needed except a decent income. The ranch provided their house, paid their electric bill, and kept their freezer full of beef. Two ranch steers went to Henry every year—he chose them himself, when they were coming off winter wheat, and then he turned them back to pasture, because, like most cowboys, he preferred the lean, sinewy meat of a range-fat steer to the rich, marbled meat of an animal fattened in a feedyard.

Still, Henry made only seven hundred dollars a month running the Willow, and most of that went out on payday just for bills and taxes. His monthly pickup allowance from the ranch gave him two hundred dollars more, but his pickup costs, for gas and bank payments, came to three hundred, and he had to add fifty dollars to meet the loan for the family car. Every winter, too, the pickup needed new tires, and they cost more than three hundred dollars. Then, there was the expense of keeping horses. The price of a colt, in a private deal, was over two hundred dollars, while a two-year-old quarter horse with some training could cost as much as seven hundred. A good saddle for that horse was another seven hundred lately; the bridle to go with it cost a hundred more, and the price of a nylon rope for roping and dragging calves was up to twenty dollars. And Henry was expected to provide the horses that he rode and to carry his own gear and saddle, just as he was expected to own the pickup that he drove. Every rancher he had ever worked for had made the assumption that cowboys took better care of their own property than somebody else's, and Henry agreed—in practice, if not in principle, his own assumption being that ranch gear was bound to be shoddy and unsafe and that ranch horses were untrustworthy. He had heard of a ranch hand down near Amarillo who had ridden out one day with a ranch bridle and suffered the rest of his life for it. The bridle was old and worn, but none of the cowboys on the ranch knew that the bit had snapped once and been welded. It snapped again that day, and the hand was thrown and trampled. Now, fourteen years and as many operations later, he was still paralyzed.

Henry had ordered his last saddle from the Stockman's Saddle Shop, in Amarillo, as a kind of compensation when Betsy started working, five years ago. His monthly pay then was only five hundred and fifty dollars, and there was never enough money to buy the groceries, keep the girls in school clothes, settle Henry's debts at the package store, and meet Betsy's Christmas Club payments at the bank. All four Blanton girls were still at home then. They wanted their own horses, and Betsy thought it would be nice if they had music lessons with the new piano teacher over in Perryton —the one who had been doing so well on the concert stage in Oklahoma City until she happened to start a conversation with a handsome cowboy in front of a statue at the National Cowboy Hall of Fame and abandoned her career for a ranch wife's life. As Betsy saw the problem, she had no choice but to take a job, and she took the first one that she was offered. Henry shouted a lot about it, and then he sulked, and finally he left the ranch one morning in the middle of work and drove straight to the sorghum dealer's office. He had been thinking, he said later, about his brother Tom, whose wife, Lisa Lou, had got herself a job in a bakery, and how humiliating it was for Tom to have to stay in the kitchen cooking lunch for everybody when he and the other hands at the Circle Y Ranch were working cattle near his camp. Henry told Betsy's boss that a cowboy's wife had her duty to her husband and to the ranch that paid him. He was eloquent. A foreman's house, he said, was a kind of command post, and a foreman's wife was like a general—well, maybe not a general but the general's

21

secretary—whose job it was to stay at that post taking messages, relaying messages, keeping track of everybody on the ranch, sending help in an emergency. He talked about the time that winter that he had had a flat tire far from home, in a freezing and remote pasture. He said that he might have died waiting out there in the cold all night if Betsy had not been home to miss him—to call the hands from their supper and tell them where to search. But the sorghum dealer was stubborn. Betsy could type and knew some shorthand, and she looked to him, he said, like a respectable woman—not like one of those town women, with their false eyelashes and skimpy skirts, who thought of a job as the free use of somebody else's telephone. Eventually, he and Henry arrived at a compromise: Betsy would work most days, but whenever Henry was working cattle at headquarters she would stay home and cook the hands a proper branding lunch.

The arrangement was fine with Betsy, whose only interest in a job anyway had been the money she would earn. That year, she gave the girls their horses, arranged for their music lessons, and bought herself a velvet pants suit with a lacy blouse for the Christmas holidays, and now, after two raises, she was making three dollars and sixty-five cents an hour and could afford a standing Saturday appointment with the hairdresser in Pampa. Still, Betsy was looking tired lately. All the cowboys' wives said so. She looked as if her life had hurt her and worn her out. Years ago, when Henry began to court her, she was the prettiest girl in her class at the district high school—a slender girl with wide blue eyes and a dimpled smile and wavy yellow hair that flipped in the wind when she went riding and was the envy of her friends.

Now there was a tension—a kind of tightness—about her. Her face had hardened under the bright, careful pouf of hair that her hairdresser said was just the thing for softening the features of tall, thin women. She was getting sallow, the way people who spend their youth outdoors turn sallow when they are shut up in closed cars and offices. And there was an anxious, bewildered look in her blue eyes when she left the house mornings and passed her husband at the chuck wagon, his black boot tapping on the spot where she suspected that his bourbon was hidden. There was something shy and tentative about those morning partings. If Henry watched the Chevrolet disappear down the cowpath and started thinking about a wife who had to go to work and shame her husband, he was apt to be edgy and dispirited by supper. He would eat too fast then, and retreat to the parlor with a copy of *TV Guide*, looking for a Western to watch on television. But if he spent the day with his head full of dreams and schemes about the future, he sat down to supper exuberant and overwrought, and then he was ready for a night in town—just like one of his Granddaddy Abel's hands on the first payday after four months out on a spring roundup.

Chapter 4

O N the evening of his fortieth birthday, Henry picked Tom up at the Circle Y Ranch and the brothers drove to Pampa. Henry was in a celebrating mood, because he had just made a birthday resolution. "It's like this, Tom," he said after they had driven in silence for half an hour, passing Henry's pickup bottle back and forth. "Here I'm getting a certain age, and I find I ain't accumulated nothing. I find . . . ."

Tom nodded.

"I mean, it was different with Daddy," Henry said. "Those old men like Daddy—they turned forty and they was just glad if they had a job. But nowadays, you turn forty —you figure you got ten, fifteen years left to really do something." Henry thought for a while. "So that's what I'm figuring to do," he said finally. "Do something."

"Shoot, Henry, we're just peons, you and me," Tom said. Tom was known for his way of putting things. He was nearly thirty-seven, but he was still all bones and joints and bashful blushes, like a boy, and when he talked, with his Adam's apple jumping around above his T-shirt collar, even his brother half expected that his voice would crack.

"Peons," Tom repeated. It was his favorite word for himself, and he liked to stretch it out in a long drawl— "peeeeons." But the fact was that Tom had been thinking about doing something, too. He had just bought an old jukebox for twenty-five dollars, and he was planning to fix it up, sell it, and, with his profit, buy two old jukeboxes, and then four, until he had bought and sold his way to a used-jukebox fortune.

When he and Henry got to town, Henry bought the first round in honor of Tom's jukebox, and Tom the next in honor of Henry's birthday resolution. They drank their bourbon and swapped stories about their best stunts. Tom played his guitar. Henry sang his favorite gospel song— "Love Lifted Me"—to anybody who would listen. And they agreed that the West was still a fine, promising place for a cowboy. They had such a good time celebrating, in fact, that when they left the bar they drove straight to a package store, with the idea of continuing in a pasture on the way home. An hour later, Henry appeared at the kitchen door of a big adobe house near Canadian, where a young ranching couple by the name of Robinson lived. His left eye was swollen shut, and he was holding Tom, who was barely conscious, in his arms.

Henry often ended up at Bay and John Robinson's house

25

when he got into trouble. His own rancher didn't bother to keep a house in the Panhandle any longer, and Tom worked for an oilman whose wife did not like cowboys coming to her house. But the Robinsons were known to be in residence—a condition that had less to do with their living on their ranch than with a kind of patron's jurisdiction. Henry admired John Robinson because John was the nearest thing he knew to the old cattle barons in the movies that he liked so much—someone on the order of, say, John Wayne in "McClintock." John Robinson was just a boy, really, who had come home from studying Greek in Cambridge, Massachusetts, to take over the family ranch from an ailing father. But John understood his duty to the whole mythic enterprise of the West, and that meant he could be counted on to shield a cowboy, speak up for a cowboy, and use his extraordinary influence, as the owner of a piece of property the size of a French province, to settle a problem quickly and quietly for a cowboy, calling on his armamentarium of doctors, lawyers, friendly policemen, and obliging judges, so that a cowboy in trouble was spared the humiliation and confusion of accounting for himself. John had taken Henry on, the way a mama cow takes on a dogie, because Henry was without a rancher of his own in residence to stand up to a sheriff or an angry wife and say, "My cowboy, right or wrong"—even when that cowboy had been in the kind of fight that left his little brother with knife slashes on his back and the skin of his right hand in shreds from plunging through the glass door of a package store.

Henry waited outside the Robinsons' kitchen, with a light spring rain pattering on his black hat, until Bay Robinson looked up from the table, where she was writing out the

26

morning's marketing list, and noticed him. Bay had been raised in Dallas, and she wore long dresses and perfume and huge pale-purple sunglasses around her house, and kept her red hair straight and shiny, like a schoolgirl's. When John first brought her to his ranch, the cowboys figured that she was one of those fluffy, fragile city girls whom ranchers' sons were fond of marrying, but Bay turned out to be a natural cowman's wife. The look that she gave Henry at the kitchen door was shrewd and maternal and amused. She helped him deposit Tom in a chair at the table, poured two drinks from a bottle of wine on the counter, and left for her library to start making phone calls. Henry sat and waited for her in the kitchen, turning his wet hat over and over in his hands and staring down at the designs on Bay's fancy Spanish floor tiles, trying to avoid the stares of the children, who came running in from their bedrooms to see what was going on. Tom, who was beginning to revive, hung his head, stuffed his tattered hand discreetly in his jacket pocket, and began hiccupping.

"Oh, no," Tom told the children. "Ain't nothing wrong with old Tom here. Just the drizzles. The drizzles plus the hiccups."

"Come on, Tom, you been up to something," Bay said, coming back in and sitting down between the brothers. She had already called her husband, who was in Oklahoma buying a supermarket chain, as well as their lawyer, their ranch manager, and one of John's business partners with clout at police headquarters. And by the time the men drove out from town for a kitchen conference she had managed to coax a look at Tom's hand, send him down the hall to change into one of John's shirts, scrub the trail of blood off

27

her floor tiles, and produce a platter of barbecued ribs for her visitors.

Henry did not talk to the three men who came to help him. He acknowledged them with a nod, and followed their hurried conversation about police and doctors less by listening than by a kind of furtive appraisal of the scene itself. He accepted an ice pack for his swollen eye, and with his other eye he watched the men, in their immaculately faded jeans and expensive Western shirts, talk about "Tom's troubles" while Tom himself sat patiently beside them, smiling bashfully and trying to eat his barbecued ribs with his left hand. From time to time, the men looked over at Henry, about to ask a question, but something about the way he stared back at them made them stop short. John's lawyer and the partner from town had been cultivating fine mustaches. They had let their hair grow long, nearly to their shoulders, and hair like that was a strong subject among Panhandle cowboys. When youngsters with long hair hitchhiked across the Panhandle in the summer on their way to communes in New Mexico, a lot of cowboys took it as a duty to pick those youngsters up, drive them off onto a lonely cowpath, and remove their hair with a razor or a knife. Henry himself had taken a few hippie scalps, as he put it. He had a lot of contempt for the people he called hippies, and now he counted John Robinson's lawyer and partner among them. Actually, he had never talked with any real hippies except a couple of ranchers' sons and the Pampa and Amarillo boys who drifted into town every now and then to pick up a few days' work at the local feedyard. But he associated hippies and their long hair with some insidious Eastern effeminacy that had infected the moral landscape of the West and left a man like him nearly help-less in his outrage. Tonight in the package store, when two long-haired strangers dressed in boots and hats and flashy Western suits took their time comparing bourbons, Henry had nudged Tom, and the two of them had taken up an old familiar litany.

"Seems like we're getting a lot of hats in this here store, Tom," Henry had started off politely.

"Yup, Henry, I'd say four hats—counting us, of course." Tom spoke so sweetly, and his smile was so shy and friendly, that one of the strangers smiled back.

"And how many hands, do you suppose, Tom?" Henry had asked him.

"Well, shoot, Henry, seems to me it takes more than a hat to make a hand."

"Now, Tom, I do believe you got a point there," Henry had said. Then he motioned toward the strangers. "I imagine our two new friends over here might just want to take them hats off."

No one had moved then except the clerk, who backed away from the counter.

"Second thought, Tom," Henry went on, "let's you and me be real nice and give these boys a hand taking off them hats."

The fight was over quickly. One of the strangers swung at Henry with a bottle. Henry kicked him back across the counter. Then the other stranger flicked open a switch-blade knife, and Tom went wild. He charged blindly, leaping and kicking and butting, and the strangers fled. They took off down the street on a pair of orange motorcycles while Tom crashed through the glass door in pursuit and

29

the clerk cried into his telephone, pleading with the lady on his party line to interrupt her nightly conversation with her married daughter so that he could call the police. Henry ran out of the store to get Tom off the sidewalk and start the pickup, but Tom was already feeling sorry about the blood and the broken bottles, and he wanted to go back in and apologize. He wanted to explain to the clerk that no one pulled a knife on Henry Blanton while Henry's little brother Tom was around. Henry had to drag him to the pickup, kicking and shouting, but finally they made their getaway. For a while, they cruised the highway, discussing what to do. There was no point in taking Tom to the hospital, where someone was sure to recognize the knife wounds on his back and report the fight to police headquarters. Then, too, Tom was modest. He would rather bleed to death than get undressed in front of a nurse, and, in fact, the last time a fight put him in the hospital he had made a fuss and insisted on sleeping in his hat and boots. There was no point in taking Tom home, either, until he was cleaned up and had a good story ready. So, a few miles past Canadian, with Tom getting weaker, Henry had turned in at the gate of the Robinsons' house. In a week or two, when Tom's hand healed, the fight tonight might enter Henry's repertoire of stories—he might brag about it then, embellishing some, until it made a dazzling stunt. But tonight Henry just sat, silent, in Bay Robinson's kitchen, looking as if he had done his duty to his brother and did not know why, suddenly, his duty seemed so humiliating to him. He waited while the men made their phone calls and Bay, setting a pan of water and some peroxide on the kitchen table, went to work cleaning Tom's hand. But when Bay noticed fresh

30

blood seeping through the back of her husband's shirt and tried to talk Tom into taking the shirt off and letting her clean his back, too, Henry spoke up for the first time and said, "I wouldn't insist, Ma'am, if I was you."

Henry left then. He simply stood up and announced that it was time he and Tom were heading home.

Bay helped him steer Tom to the door. "Come on now, Henry," she whispered. "What were you boys up to?"

"Just celebrating, Ma'am," Henry said.

Chapter 5

Grass was cheap when Henry's Granddaddy Abel passed through the Panhandle on a cattle drive and decided to send for a bride, settle down on some land of his own, and become a cattle baron. Texans were buying up good pastureland for just a few dollars an acre in those days, and there was still so much land left over that the state was able to offer sixteen free square-mile sections in exchange for every mile of track surveyed and laid on its new railroads. In fact, the railroad surveyors were even able to stretch a mile some on those occasions, so that a railroader or his client could often count on ending up with six hundred and eighty acres in each of his free sections, while a homesteader, getting *his* land from the Texas school trust, had to settle for a normal six hundred and forty. In Abel Blanton's day, spending land saved people the expense of spending money. Abel knew a man from the old town of Mobeetie who had lost a hundred dollars in a poker game and, being low on cash that night, had paid the winner twenty-five thousand acres instead. Then, there was the time the legislators in Austin decided they had to have a state capitol with a big and impressive dome like the one in Washington they heard so much about. They voted to save the construction cost by offering three million acres of the Panhandle to anybody who would build it for them. Some English businessmen heard about the offer from a firm of Chicago contractors, and ended up with a ranch that was forty-five miles wide in most places and ran a hundred and ninety-five miles down the state's western border, from the top of the Panhandle toward the Rio Grande.

The Englishmen called their ranch the XIT. The name supposedly stood for Ten in Texas—the ranch took in the better part of ten counties—and it gave them a brand that was complicated enough to be practically guaranteed against a rustler's running irons. There was always work for a good hand on the XIT. Henry's grandfather took a job there for a few years while he saved money for a down payment on his own spread. He was scrupulous about saving. He kept his cash in a saddlebag and rode with it on roundups, and every payday that he was home he had his wife, Clara, count it. Clara Blanton was a preacher's daughter, and, unlike Abel, she could read and write. Her prize possession was a big household ledger, which she took out of the family trunk on money-counting days and read for sustenance, the way she read the Bible, while Abel emptied his saddlebag on their cabin floor. Her ledger stayed in the family trunk until the nineteen-fifties, when a tornado hit Henry's parents' house and blew the trunk away. Henry had discovered it as a boy and was both scandalized and delighted to learn that his Granddaddy Abel already had two thousand dollars in his saddlebag when he started work at the XIT. The money was a kind of commission on the strays that Abel had rustled and rebranded for the group of small south-Texas ranchers who shared his services as a trail boss. Mavericks were a good sideline for a cowboy during Abel's first years on the trail—Henry used to complain that the only real difference between him and some of the big cattlemen he knew was that *their* grandfathers had got away with more mavericks—but by the time Abel decided to settle down in the Panhandle business had fallen off. Brands were registered by then and checked en route to the railheads and checked again at auction. And, as Abel once put it, a stray calf lost a lot of its appeal when you knew that all the big ranchers moving cattle were paying five or six hired guns, whom they called "trail representatives" and everybody else called "enforcers." Wages were low on the XIT, but the work was dependable. Abel did well there. He was a man reformed by dreams of property. He had lost his faith back in Georgia, but now, in Texas, he welcomed Christ again, and even made some extra money into the bargain, holding Baptist revival meetings on the local ranch circuit. Four years later, in 1896, he had four thousand dollars in his saddlebag. It made a down payment on six sections of good grazing land, at the going price of two dollars and fifty cents an acre, and the rest of the money that he needed came from a rich German farmer, whose first homestead crop had been burned by a band of cowboy vigilantes, and who was taking his revenge slowly, making short-term loans at twenty-five per cent interest to cowboys with excellent prospects of defaulting.

Some of the best and smartest cowboys Henry Blanton knew were sons or grandsons of hands like Abel, who had tried to become ranchers and lost everything in the process, but it was hard for even the smartest cowboys to accept the fact that ranching in the Old West had been as much a rich man's gamble as it was now. They knew, of course, that ranchers today had to have a lot of capital. There were big corporation ranches in the Panhandle that ran according to elaborate cost-plus systems of accounting —systems that could turn a bad cattle year profitable in terms of tax savings to the corporation as a whole—but the successful independent ranchers almost always had enough money behind them to cover their losses and keep them going through a droughty year or a glutted market, a sorghum shortage or a drop in cattle futures, a change in beef-grading regulations, or even a housewives' boycott at the butcher's, like the one in 1973, just after President Richard Nixon's price freeze.

Ranching lately had less to do with an individual's adventure with a herd of cattle than with that global network of dependencies and contingencies that people had taken to calling "agribusiness." Henry liked to say that the only people he knew with a taste for simple, range-fat steers were the cowboys who got theirs free. The packers, the wholesalers, and the public demanded an animal that had put in time on fodder feed. That animal might have feasted on buckets of homegrown corn in a barn in Iowa on its way to a fancy butcher or an expensive steak house, or it might have spent the last four months of its short life in a feedyard pen with fifty thousand other animals, all of them destined for frozen dinners or cheap hamburger stands. But, either way, in a year like 1972—the year the Russians concluded their famous and mysterious deal for the country's wheat and corn surplus and the price of those grains at home started rising—the rancher who owned that animal could lose everything unless he had the cash or the credit to see him through.

A lot of the small postwar ranchers in the Panhandle were lucky enough to have made a quick oil or gas strike on their land and assured themselves of backup capital. Most of the big modern ranchers already had their oil or their gas, their banks or their board chairmanships, before they bought a single cow. One of the best of them—a rancher by the name of Jay Taylor—also happened to own forty per cent of the Amarillo Livestock Auction Company, which eventually became the biggest cattle-auction company in the country, with a turnover, at one per cent commissions, of more than half a million head in a good year. Then, there were the young Marsh brothers, Stanley, Tom, and Michael, who, along with what they made on natural gas and banks and television stations and a dozen other ventures, could always count on money from the federal government, because their family ranch happened to sit on a natural underground dome, some ten miles wide, that the government liked to use for storing four-fifths of the Western world's entire helium reserves. Some of the big ranching families started poor. Jay Taylor's grandfather was a trail boss, like Abel Blanton. But few of those families made their first million ranching, and the ones that did usually

36

had someone else's money behind them. There was a joke in the Panhandle about a rancher with a hundred thousand acres and four thousand fine Hereford breeder cows. One day, the rancher sold his house and his Continental and resigned from the country club. "My oil well's run dry," he told his friends sadly. "I'll have to go back to depending on my cattle."

There were no oil wells or gas wells in the Panhandle when Abel Blanton bought his six sections. The first natural gas was tapped in 1918 by a local company, the Amarillo Oil Company, that had been drilling for oil and, to everyone's disappointment, brought in a ten-million-cubic-foot gas deposit. Gulf tapped the first Panhandle oil three years later, after drilling some three thousand feet for it. The countryside was still wild in Abel's time. Ranch children foraged for wild plums and grapes in the Palo Duro Canyon. There were big junipers—long gone now—in the canyon, and bears and pumas roamed the Canadian breaks. Earlier settlers had pushed to the edge of the Panhandle, moving east from the old Spanish colonies in New Mexico and north from the rest of Texas, but aside from a couple of boom towns like Amarillo the Panhandle itself was barely inhabited.

The Panhandle was Indian country until 1874. Comanche had taken over the area after 1700, and they kept it for themselves for the next hundred and fifty years, letting in only some Cheyenne and Kiowa. They drove back the Spanish herders who had been grazing their sheep, summers, by the Canadian River. They raided frontier towns for horses, which they kept, and for captives, whom they sold to enterprising Mexicans for guns, whiskey, and colored cloth. And they saw to it that not many white men wanted to enter the Panhandle with Comanche there. Occasionally, Spanish and then Mexican soldiers from garrisons in Santa Fe or San Miguel del Bado came on reprisal raids, and so did a few intrepid whiskey traders. Kit Carson arrived for an Indian war in 1864, but the first whites who actually came with the intention of staying were the buffalo hunters, and they did not arrive until 1873—which was the year they seem to have discovered that the Army's much-vaunted Indian-treaty "policy" of keeping white hunters north of the Arkansas River was little more than a rumor. The buffalo hunters had nine months before the Indians took them on, in the famous raid that Texas history books call the Battle of Adobe Walls. The United States Cavalry, in turn, took on the Indians, chasing their warriors back and forth across the Panhandle until the Indians, demoralized and exhausted, surrendered themselves to reservation life. After that, the cattlemen came in.

The first proper rancher was a man from Illinois named Charles Goodnight, who, like Abel Blanton, had made his living driving cattle north from south Texas—selling the cattle to reservations or at auctions in Colorado. Goodnight came to the Panhandle to stay in 1876. He started out in a two-room log cabin, and one of the reasons cowboys like Abel dreamed of becoming rich cowmen was that Charlie Goodnight, in his tiny cabin, became one. Actually, Goodnight had found himself a rich British backer—one with the money to finance the purchase of a million acres and run a hundred thousand head of cattle. The backer's name was John George Adair. He was an investment banker with his eye on the American West, where the re-

turns on venture capital were already greater than anywhere in Europe, and Goodnight, passing through Denver
on a cattle drive, had come across Adair's agent and talked
him into a loan. Goodnight borrowed thirty thousand dollars from John Adair, and eventually had the use of Adair's
considerable credit, but he paid eighteen per cent interest
on that thirty thousand, and in 1877, when they formed a
partnership, Goodnight had to run their JA Ranch for five
years, at a small salary, before he could claim his third of
the property.

Most of the early Panhandle ranches were financed, like
the JA, by English or Scottish capitalists. Their agents
would sit in rocking chairs on the porch of the big new
yellow hotel—the Amarillo Hotel—on the corner of Polk
and Third Streets and hold court for the ranchers and
cowboys and cattle traders who hitched their horses to the
Amarillo's wooden posts, hoping to make the deal that
would change their lives. For years, the Amarillo was the
agents' local headquarters; anyone who wanted to do business in the Panhandle took a room. The hotel belonged to
H. B. Sanborn, a prototype developer who once, in fact,
owned the entire town. Sanborn had come to the Panhandle in the eighteen-eighties to promote J. F. Glidden's Wire
Fence, which was the infamous twisted "wire that fenced
the West"—the first successful barbed wire to be mass-
produced. Joseph Glidden, the inventor, held the patent on
the design, but Sanborn, as his agent, did so well on commissions that he and Glidden's son-in-law, William Bush,
were able to buy up two hundred square miles of the Panhandle, ostensibly to test the wire against the battering of
wild Texas longhorns. Bush actually used his share of the

39

land for ranching, but Sanborn was at heart a speculator, and the wildest speculation in west Texas in the eighteen-eighties was in towns—which towns would get the railroad, which towns would get the votes of the local cowhands and become important county seats. People were buying a few empty sections, throwing together enough buildings to make the place look settled, and then maneuvering to put the people with the "town" next door out of business. In 1889, Sanborn was trying to get the Potter County seat moved east by a mile and onto his own property, and he was consequently doing a lot of fast building, along with paying people in the old township to drag their houses on sled runners to Sanborn land. The Amarillo Hotel was his coup. He meant it to be a Panhandle institution, and by Abel Blanton's day it had lived up to his intention. It was stocked —as Sanborn used to say before he lost a lot of his money speculating—with the loosest women, the strongest whiskey, and the trickiest cardplayers in five hundred miles.

Abel Blanton did not approve of the goings on at the Amarillo. A lost war and a hard life had left him with a touch of melancholia. He was rigid and austere, and proud of it, and his new enthusiasm for the details of eternal fire had put the fear of God into quite a number of cowboys' children on his Sunday-morning ranch circuit. But after one droughty summer on his six sections—a summer of trying to keep a hundred cows and their calves alive, and of fretting about his debt to the German farmer, who figured in Abel's nightmares as a fat, fire-snorting Catholic devil—he rode the eighty miles from his ranch to Amarillo and presented himself at the Amarillo Hotel. He stayed for three days waiting for an audience with the porch money men, but the audience never happened. His only offer came from a local rancher, who gave him a night's lodging on the way home and told him in the morning to stop back about a foreman's job if he should ever happen to lose his land.

Abel kept his ranch going for ten more years. He sold twenty of his cows one year to meet his payments to the German farmer. The next year, he sold his best section. After that, he tried everything he could think of. For a while, he raised mules; then he leased two sections to a farmer, and with the money he paid off his loan. He had a few good years before the winter of 1918 ruined him. Two of his children had died of flu that fall, and he and Clara and the other children nearly died with them. There was snow that winter, too. The storms were the worst in anybody's memory, and by January of 1919 there were drifts of twenty and thirty feet in Abel's pastures. Some of his cows starved to death. Some froze. As soon as Abel was strong enough to leave his cabin, he rode out, his chest rubbed down with Clara's special liniment of camphor, bacon grease, and coal oil, and rounded up the cattle that were left. Not many of his cows could walk by then, after a month of hunger and punishing snowstorms. Abel had to cart them on makeshift sleds some forty miles to the nearest railhead, and then he waited for a week, camping in the snow, for a rescue train, shipped his cows to the nearest market, and took what he could get for them.

Abel sold his last few sections for not much more than he had paid for them. He loaded his household goods in three wagons and, with his family, his milk cows, and a few mules, headed across the Panhandle to find the rancher who ten years earlier had offered him a job. Abel was fifty-two then. He was still working for the same rancher when he died, at ninety. For years, he brooded on his failure, convinced that God had punished him for some great wickedness involving his three-day stay in Amarillo. No one in the family knew precisely what that wickedness had been, but they all dutifully accompanied Abel Blanton to town one fall day in 1925, renounced the Baptist Church with him, and one by one jumped into a tub of freezing water to be born again in the Church of Christ, which held that Baptist dunkings were not sufficient in the matter of remitting sins. The Church of Christ also held that, whatever the Baptists might say about "once saved, always saved," a man could fall from grace, sinning, any day of his Christian life —and that was something that appealed to Abel Blanton. Thinking about sin turned him cheerful, and even humorous, in his middle age. Henry knew old cowpunchers who still remembered Abel preaching from his wagon on a spring roundup. "You got to do right!" Abel always shouted. And then, chuckling away and pounding on his mess-kit pan, he would shout louder, "Ignorance ain't going to save you, 'cause it don't matter a damn to God if you been misinformed!"

Abel was a hard foreman on a roundup. He thought of liquor as Satan's water. He would fire a hand who rode out with a bottle, and none of his hands could sing or play their guitars or harmonicas, because Abel didn't approve of music, either. Not many of Abel's hands were churchgoing men. They left religion to their wives and children and boasted a lot about belonging to the church of the great outdoors, but they kept a kind of respect for Abel, because he was, after all, a fine old cowpuncher. Some of them even enjoyed his preaching. Once, when Henry was nine and was out with Abel for the first time on a roundup, there was a long argument about harmonicas. One of the hands got up and said that, as he saw it, there was no harm in playing a harmonica, since God encouraged harps and trumpets and most likely harmonicas, too, in Heaven. Abel Blanton waved a hand at the range around him and said, "This ain't Heaven."

Chapter 6

HENRY and his brother Tom were out behind the barn at Henry's headquarters, and there were two Willow cowboys, Calvin Pratt and Ed Loomis, with them. Tom had been stopping by mornings to pass the time while his hand healed. It was seven-thirty now. Two hundred and eleven calves were lowing in a big wooden pen that opened onto the chute to the calf cradle, but Henry wanted to wait for Sam Otis before he gave the word to start them down the chute. Sam was an old cowpuncher who had lived and worked on a neighboring ranch for so many years that people long ago stopped calling the ranch by name and began saying simply "Sam's place." There was a younger man in Sam's old camp now, and Sam had been retired, as his foreman put it, to a one-room shack in town, which he shared with a wife reputed to be the mean-est-tempered woman in the county. He was very ill. He had survived two heart operations in the past year, and his fear was terrible, but it was not so much a fear of death that hounded Sam as a fear of his own uselessness as a cowhand. Lately, a morning's job at the Willow was enough to keep him plucky and boasting for a week. Work was the only thing that cheered Sam, and Henry tried to send for him whenever a batch of Okie calves came in and he could use an extra hand—a child would do—to sit on the chute rail with a charged hotshot and prod them toward the cradle.

The cowboys waited, stretched out in the shadow of the barn with a tin of Copenhagen snuff on the grass between them, while Henry talked to his brother about a deal with Lester Hill, his ranch manager, that was going to make his fortune. Lester had driven up one day last week to check on a requisition for a ton of feed cake, and Henry, remembering his birthday resolution, decided that the time had come for them to have a talk. He was careful not to say anything about the one per cent of last year's gross that he knew was due him as the ranch foreman—a lot of Panhandle ranchers were giving percentage bonuses to their best cowboys, and Henry had not seen a bonus for the past five years. He had not expected much from those years, because of all the trouble in the cattle business. Even now, most ranchers around did well if they were breaking even, but, still, Henry calculated that Lester was holding back some four thousand dollars—and Henry might have said so if asking for money had not been painful for him. There were other jobs around. Henry knew of one foreman's job, at a big ranch just across the Oklahoma border, that paid eight hundred dollars a month, and came with health insurance and a pension plan, and offered twice the average gasoline allowance, because the nearest high school was forty-five miles from the ranch gate. But he had not mentioned the job, either. He had simply sat down next to Lester in the front seat of Lester's air-conditioned Buick and, after a respectable silence, announced that he was thinking of quitting. And after another respectable silence Lester had offered him a deal to stay. It was a kind of partnership, really, in a batch of Okie calves that Lester had bought, with a bank loan, through an agent in Louisiana. Henry was going to look after those calves for a season. He was going to run them with the ranch cattle, and in return he and Lester would split the profits when the calves were sold.

"Seems to me you run a lot of Lester's cattle without him giving you a nickel for it," Tom said after Henry had told his story.

"Maybe he's reformed," Henry said, frowning with concentration. He had his pad out, and he was busy calculating the profit on a hundred calves, bought cheap, grazed well, and sold at the Amarillo Livestock Auction with a lot of water bringing up their weight. He was going to put his share toward another hundred head, then two hundred. In a few years, he would have the cash for a down payment on a few sections of his own.

"Seems to me jukeboxes is a lot cheaper," Tom said. His own jukebox was waiting in the barn at the Circle Y, but there was no way for him to work on it with a bandaged hand.

"I'm going to find me a backer," Henry told him. "Maybe a rich lady from New York. I saw on television the other

46

night that them Eastern ladies got control of all their husbands' money."

Calvin Pratt shook his head. Calvin did not approve of Henry or his cattle deal. He was Henry's best hand and could have been foreman of a ranch himself, but he was at heart a farmer, not a cowboy. He loved to see the dirt turned, to pick it up and smell it, to sit on a tractor and watch things grow. He was fifty years old, and he had tried three times to keep a small vegetable-and-alfalfa farm going. A drought ruined him the first time. Then he was drafted and sent to fight in the Korean war. His last farm failed when old debts and his own poverty caught up with him. He had turned to cowboying then, with a grim and deliberate acquiescence. Even now, years later, there was still a spare, proud homesteader's quality about Calvin—about the way he dressed for work, in his slim brown jeans with the creases always pressed fresh, his narrow belt and plain brown walking boots and buff hat; about the way he walked and rode and clipped a fence wire, and even rolled a cigarette. It gave him a kind of elegance. His gestures were patient and precise, and his only passion, as far as any of the men knew, was coyotes. At night, when the coyotes howled, Calvin liked to drive out after them in his pickup with his three dogs, Sam, Steve, and Seoul. He carried a rifle on the pickup, but he rarely used it. He preferred to sit smoking cigarettes and watch his dogs cut a coyote from its pack and tear the animal apart.

Calvin glanced back at the penned calves. They were scrawny and scabby. Most of them looked sick. They had just spent two days in a filthy sale barn in Louisiana and another day, at least, in a cattle truck without food or water, and now some were slavering and others scouring. Cowboys called their sickness "shipping fever"—it was a way of covering a disease syndrome that usually cost more to identify than a calf was worth. "I reckon it's some of these fine young calves that's going to make Henry here a millionaire," Calvin said.

"Shoot, Calvin," Tom said. "According to that television show I seen the other night—it was about them I.Q. tests —we can all get to be millionaires. 'Cause we're so in-tell-i-gent. Least, that's what the show said. It said them I.Q. tests we all took back there in school—why, they don't count none." Tom grinned slyly. "Now, I sure was glad to hear that. Shoot, I used to think I was pretty ignorant, just a peon. So I sure am glad to know I'm so sensible."

"Well, it takes less sense to be a cowboy than any other profession I ever did hear of," Calvin said. "You don't think. You just go out, do what you're told, go to work— unless you're old Henry here, and can lay around giving orders."

Henry stood up and stretched, and then he started unloading the bed of an old pickup that he kept behind the barn as a kind of open toolshed. There was an icebox propped up in the truck. Henry emptied it, tossing a jar of sulfa pills and a couple of injection guns down to Ed Loomis and then jumping down himself with four big bottles of calf vaccine in his arms. Calvin, meanwhile, had poured some disinfectant over a sponge in a rusty pot and was cleaning his knife on it. There was nothing left to do but hook up the Willow branding iron to a charged battery and wait for Sam.

"I sure do wish we had known all that when we was

younger—I mean about them I.Q. tests being wrong," Ed said, pounding Tom on the back and laughing. Ed was in a fine mood this morning—he always was when he was working cattle. There was a dazed cheerfulness about the way he took a saw or a pair of spoon pliers to a calf's horns that frightened some people and made others think that he was either feeble or a little crazy. He had a reputation for wildness, but he looked up to Henry; and Henry, enjoying the admiration, kept him on, and even took his side when he got into trouble. Henry liked to say that Ed's wife was to blame for his peculiarities. She had taken their two small boys five years ago and left him for a job in a shoe store in Oklahoma—with a promise to drive home on weekends to clean the kitchen and do the wash. For a time, she kept her promise, but over the years she had gradually stopped coming—it was a year and a half since anyone on the ranch had seen her—and Ed, who pined for his wife and sons and rode with their picture in a gummy cellophane folder in his jeans pocket, had gradually got slaphappy with a saw or a knife or a branding iron in his hand. He lived with another cowboy now, in a trailer that was parked in a pasture seven miles from headquarters, and he kept his horse and his gear in an old refrigerator car off the Santa Fe Railway. Being unsuitable, as Henry put it, for looking after ranch cows and their babies, Ed had got the job of looking after the ranch Mississipps. It was plain that no one was looking after Ed. He lived on cans of Beanee Weenees—beans with a bit of sausage. A lot of his teeth were gone, and the ones he had were brown from neglect and chewing tobacco. There was usually a week's growth of greasy stubble on his face. He owned a pair of frayed chaps, which he always wore, whatever the work or the weather, along with a reeking T-shirt and worn jeans. "Yup, I do wonder what we would have 'mounted to if we'd known how educated we really was," Ed said. "I seem to remember that there I.Q. test saying I shouldn't go to work in one of them offices."

"Well, *I* did get above what I was supposed to be," Calvin said. "Least, for a time I did."

"Course, there's nothing lower than a cowboy," Tom volunteered.

Henry, who was feeding black-leg serum into one of the injection guns, looked up at Tom. "You remember that time I took the test?" he said.

Tom nodded, and the rest of the men stopped talking.

"You had to say what was a domesticated animal," Henry went on. "So I put 'rabbit,' seeing as how I had a rabbit. And then that old teacher of mine, she said that was pretty dumb—she said anybody could see that 'dog' was the proper answer." Henry shook his head. "But you *could* call a rabbit domesticated if it's *been* domesticated." He shook his head again. "I mean, if there'd been somebody telling me I was right, I might of got encouraged. I might of studied something important—something like accounting or that economics deal, 'cause that's what you need nowadays if you're going to run a ranch right."

Calvin wiped his knife across the sponge, thoughtful, while Tom sucked on a piece of grass and Ed, grinning mindlessly at them all, scratched his stomach.

"I mean, this cattle business—there's a new market every day," Henry said. He was pacing back and forth in front of the calf cradle, pink with shame and caught up in his own bravado. "It's what's on them ticker tapes that counts. It's

50

high finance, and if a man's out working with his hands, there's no telling how much he's going to be losing. No, sir, he has to be right in front of that machine of his, finding out what's happening in New York City. Otherwise, he's going to end up nothing but some other man's dumb cowboy."

"Cowboy? What cowboy?" Sam Otis appeared behind the barn, riding on a bony old palomino quarter horse that he called Thunder and the hands inevitably addressed as Horsemeat. It was a matter of pride with Sam to arrive for work on horseback. On a day like today, he would hitchhike out from town to the ranch gate, pick up the jeep that Melinda used to meet her school bus, and drive it back to headquarters—and then he would tiptoe into the barn to saddle Thunder and make the last hundred feet of his trip in style. Henry expected his hands to greet Sam as if the old man had been riding hard since dawn.

"Seems to me you got to distinguish between different types of cowboys," Sam said. "There's rodeo cowboys, dude cowboys, feedyard cowboys, stockyard cowboys—and then there's real cowboys."

"You mean peon cowboys," Tom said, giving Sam a leg down.

"I mean the kind that wouldn't change none for a million dollars. Take me—I wanted to punch cows. That's all I ever wanted to do, and that's what I always done."

"You better put down drinking whiskey on that list." Tom grinned, plucking a pint from Sam's jacket pocket.

Sam ignored him. He was looking over at the day's calves. "Maybe they ain't so sick as they look," he said finally.

51

"It's a bad business, running these poor calves," Calvin said. Usually, Calvin worked with the Willow cow herd. He liked animals that were clean and hardy and bred scientifically, as he put it. This new business of speculating on strangers' cattle that arrived in trucks, grazed for a season, and then disappeared into feedyards seemed unnatural to him. Lately, the Mississipps had been coming and going so fast and so frequently that it was easy for a manager like Lester Hill, with his boss across an ocean, to slip a shipment of his own down the chute and onto one of the ranch pastures. The last time that calves with Lester's ear tag on them arrived in a truckload of ranch cattle, Calvin had driven off, indignant, to his own camp, saying that Lester Hill's cattle were not his job.

"Well, there's none of us that *like* this," Henry said, setting his injection guns down on a broken chair beside the calf cradle. He was uneasy lately, and embarrassed around Calvin. Last night, he had considered inviting him for a drink in town after supper and then maybe offering him a cut, but he had given up on that idea before he even reached the telephone. Calvin never went drinking. He spent his evenings in a pine rocker in his parlor, dressed up in a clean shirt and his good boots, and working jigsaw puzzles while his wife, Annabel, read the Bible or wrote letters to their married son. Annabel went to Bible class with Betsy on Sunday mornings, and once, in class, she had told Betsy that Calvin had suffered from "a little depression problem" after they had lost their last farm. Annabel had asked God to solve that problem, and she had promised, in return, to inspire her husband to a life of domestic happiness. She kept her lipstick fresh and her hair curled and her house spotless. Cowboys were permitted in her kitchen, but no cowboy sat down on the flowered chintz cushions in Annabel's parlor unless it was Sunday and he was paying a visit with his wife.

"I'd say here's four men what don't like working with these chutes," Sam said. He was perched on a rail now, poking some calves down the chute with his hotshot. Henry clamped the first calf into the cradle while Ed slammed the headhold into place for him, and then they tipped the cradle on its side. Calvin spread the calf's hind legs with an iron rod. Working together, the three men had the calf branded, dehorned, castrated, injected, and hobbling off to pasture in about a minute. Henry gave the shots today, Ed pried the horns off, and Calvin cut and branded. Tom, who had disappeared into the barn, came back with a bucket for Sam Otis. Sam always got the testicles at a branding. He traded them for whiskey at a restaurant in Pampa that specialized in deep-fried mountain oysters as an appetizer.

Sam chuckled. "The only thing that's the same about this business here and roping and dragging cattle is them oysters and the bottle of bourbon. Course, you do need eight or ten people when you work a-horseback."

"Hard to find ten people nowadays," Tom said. "There's not so many want to work cheap, like we do. And working them calves on the ground is harder—least to me."

"But you get to do what you know how to do," Henry said. "This way—well, to me it's like being on one of them factory lines. It's boring." In a minute, he added, "This makes near three thousand calves we put through the chute since January."

"Well, I can't see why a rancher that's been a millionaire

all his life and has a fine herd of cows dropping babies every year—I sure can't understand what makes him want to go fooling round with these critters," Sam said. "And as for dragging calves—I don't think it's any harder on them than squeezing them into these contraptions."

"It really depends on how you been treating them all along," Calvin said, frowning. There was a new calf in the cradle now, scouring and frothing as Ed sawed wildly on its horns. Calvin worked quickly, and then, with the branding iron still sizzling in his hand, he ran to the headhold and began to stroke the calf's forehead. "There, there, you poor little old thing," he murmured. "That's the worst, that saw. That hurts you more than anything, don't it?"

Ed finished one horn. He poured a dose of Anchor Blood Stopper powder on the stump and wiped the blood off his T-shirt with a rag from his pocket. Then he slammed a bar across the calf's nose. "Goddammit, this'll keep you steady," he said, and he laughed and laughed.

Sam ran up to him. "Easy now, Ed."

Ed started on the second horn. Blood shot into the air and came down on everyone.

Henry started shouting. "Ed! Hey, Ed! Ain't you cutting a little deep?" And then, "Ed, come on!"

"You must of been hitting the jug pretty early." Sam shook his hotshot like a stick. "You want them calves to bleed to death?"

"Yeah," Tom said. "If you're going to skin them, use a knife, not a saw."

Henry waited for a moment. Then he swung himself up onto the truck chassis and crawled around, cursing, until he had found a long red plunger hidden under a pile of tools.

It took a while, but he finally managed to force a sulfa tablet down the calf's throat. Calvin stood by, murmuring and stroking, and Ed watched, laughing softly to himself.

After that, Henry called a break.

"I tell you, it ain't like the old times, and it hurts this old cowpuncher's heart to see it," Sam told him later. The men were resting, and Sam and Henry had walked over to a deep trench—a cattle-dipping vat—that ran behind the corral, and were having a drink from Sam's bottle. The trench was dry and littered with old tools and bottles and rusty horseshoes. The sight of it always made Sam nostalgic—it reminded him of a summer in the nineteen-thirties when all the cows had scabies and Sam had had to run fifteen thousand head through the dipping vat on his old ranch. Not many ranchers used their dipping vats anymore. It cost two hundred dollars these days to charge a vat the size of the Willow's with enough water and insecticide for a run of only five hundred animals, and Henry's orders for the past few years had been to save money and spray his cattle with insecticide instead. The calves that he was working now had been sprayed yesterday, getting off the truck, but there were still ticks on every one of them.

"You know when it all began to change?" Sam said. He spat a wad of snuff into the trench, and he and Henry headed back toward the calves. The men got up, stretching and spitting, and took their places at the cradle. "It was when that Roosevelt fella got in," Sam said. "That was the end—that P.W.A., or whatever they call it. Boy, I'd of died before I got on one of them welfare things. Your old cowpuncher—he's got a little pride. He don't want no one taking care of him. But these young ones, they work three days and then they quit and go into town and expect the government to feed them. They never do want to help out none"—Sam climbed onto the chute rail and jabbed a bucking calf toward the cradle—"so it's no wonder we got to have these contraptions. Where are you going to find ten good hands that wants to put in a day's work riding and roping? Where're you going to find *one* good hand nowadays that's willing to put up with the weather, riding all night, like I did, when it's raining like blazes, or roping in the hot sun, or—"

"Seems to me if I was to quit tomorrow there'd be ten men lined up and ready to take my job," Calvin put in, but then he shrugged. "Not that they'd be qualified."

Henry was thinking. He opened the cradle and slapped the calf out to pasture, nodding and frowning at his own thoughts. "Seems to me like we been kind of breaking nature's law," he said finally. "I mean, the law of nature is for the strongest to survive, ain't it? But here we kind of take care of the weakest. Now, don't get me wrong. I don't mind the weakest. I mind the ones with no ambition. Them old cowpunchers in the movies—they got what they wanted 'cause of ambition. Else they worked for somebody who knew how to use them. You got to see old Chill Wills in 'The Rounders' to know what those old cattlemen were really like. Chill Wills—he had these cowboys, and they'd stay out in the country so long on one of them old round-ups that when they got their pay and went to town, boy, it was like they was never going back. They'd get in trouble all right in town, and then old Chill Wills, he'd just drive in and bail them out and . . ."

Calvin shook his head, puzzled.

"You see, then they'd *have* to go back out to work for him." Henry aimed an injection gun filled with Vitamin A and penicillin. "All them psychology doctors and professors—they don't know half of what old Chill Wills knew. I mean, how to get things out of people and still make them feel such a part. Course, nowadays, most places, if a man don't want to work there's nothing his boss can do about it, because all that man has to do is call his union, and before you know it his old boss ain't got *no one* working for him."

"There's some people says there ought to be a cowboys' union," Tom said, and then he slapped his knee with his good hand and rolled back on the ground laughing.

"Now, ain't that a good one!" Sam said.

"Well, they did have them a union down at old Tascosa once," Tom said, sitting up again. "The way I heard it, the boys got drunk and called a strike, and the cowmen just let them strike until they got so hungry they had to go back to work."

"That was near a hundred years ago," Sam said.

"You know what them cowmen called their hands?" Tom asked him. "Cow servants!" Tom chuckled. "Why, I believe that's the same as peons."

Henry scowled. "They weren't real cowmen. They was Englishmen."

"Anyhow, they had these hands—twenty-four or twenty-five cowboys—and, like old Sam said, it was near a hundred years ago, and them poor old cowboys was making thirty dollars a month, working every day, day and night. So the boys got drunk one night, down in Tascosa—"

Calvin shook his head. "That ain't it at all. They had this

headquarters in Tascosa. And the ranchers tried to burn them out. That's the way *I* heard it. Them ranchers drove to town in a buckboard with a barrel of gunpowder. They was all hiding behind the buckboard, arguing about who was going to light that fuse. There wasn't one of them as wasn't scared to show himself. They had to get this old nigger cook to come out and light the fuse for them."

"The way *I* heard it, they killed the strike leader," Sam said. "Poisoned him. And told the sheriff that he was like one of them hippies—said he died from drugs. Opium, or whatever it was they had back then."

All the men were quiet.

"Well, you won't see none of us giving up our freedom to join no union," Henry said.

Everybody nodded, solemn.

"Damn right," Sam said. "With them unions—you know, the union says don't take that job, and you can't take it, not even if you're starving. I say the hell with that."

"Sam's right," Henry said. "We may not be as well off as some financially, but we're more independent."

"Not old Calvin here," Sam said, chuckling. "He ain't independent. Annabel's been henpecking him for years."

Calvin kept on branding.

"Well, Calvin?" Tom said.

"Least I can say that Annabel ain't no liberated woman. Annabel ain't never run off and worked, like some I know."

Henry stiffened.

"Well, you might say that about my Lisa Lou," Tom said cheerfully. "Why, if it was my camp today, you'd be getting Beanee Weenees for lunch instead of fried steak and gravy. But Betsy—seems to me Betsy's one of them women that's been liberated against her wishes. You don't hear her griping none about her privileges."

Ed grinned. "I hear them liberated women don't want no separate rest rooms. Well, I say fine. Let them fight in the wars, too. Let them have the same jails as what the men have. Let them play football—"

"I agree with Ed here," Calvin said. "Let them do the same as men do if they want to be liberated. Let them work in a foundry, put them out on the range digging postholes."

Tom looked horrified. "Come on, Calvin. I believe there's some things, like digging postholes—well, a woman wasn't made to do that. And, shoot, she shouldn't have to. The way I see it, if she does the same job as a man, she should be paid the same and treated fair, that's all. My wife come home the other day and said she wasn't treated fair at work, and it just made me mad."

Calvin shook his head. "Don't know where she got the idea that everybody's going to treat you fair and equal in this life."

"There's some women complain about a man sitting down to lunch with a little blood on him," Ed put in, looking down at his T-shirt. "Hell, I wouldn't want no woman to be cussing at me all the time."

"See that tree, Ed?" Tom said. He pointed to a fine old cottonwood over by the pen. It was heavy with ripe seeds, just bursting into bloom. "That's real pretty, ain't it?"

"Another month and that cotton will be blowing every which way," Calvin remarked.

Ed waited.

"What I mean is this," Tom said, blushing. "You know

what they say about this life being no more than—now, what is it that they say?—no more than a flower blooming. Well, that's what I believe. There's just no point wasting time complaining and haggling over things that is."

Sam, on the rail, whooped with glee. "Save your breath, Tom. Once them Russians take over, they ain't going to *permit* no haggling. And them Russians *is* going to take over, 'cause that's what happens when you take people's guns away, like they're fixing to do back there in Austin. That's what we pay them legislators for—six hundred dollars a month, I heard it was."

"And thirty a day expenses," Calvin said.

"For lying and talking nonsense and taking guns away so a man can't shoot a robber or a bad nigger or one of them Communists." Sam was so excited that he nearly tumbled off the rail. "I tell you, that's the day them Russians is going to just walk in and take over, knowing we got no guns to defend ourselves."

Henry called for the next calf. The sun was high now, and hot, and there were still a hundred calves in the pen to brand by lunchtime. The cowboys, exhausted, took their places at the cradle. They seemed to move through a film of dust and sweat and blood.

Calvin cut the calf, frowning.

"Look at it this way, Calvin," Tom said gently. "Like you're doing a little neighboring for old Henry here this morning."

"Every cowboy wants his own cattle," Sam said. "Yup, his own cattle and a pair of handmade boots. It's been twenty years since I had me a pair of handmade boots."

"Every cowboy wants his own land, too," Calvin said.

60

"You think they'd learn, since I never seen but one or two who did get it."

Ed picked up his saw, looking thoughtful. "It sure is true that there's more cowboys than rich people," he said finally.

Henry slammed the cradle shut on the next calf and said, "We ain't got all day."

Chapter 7

Last year, Americans ate twenty-seven billion pounds of beef—a hundred and twenty-nine pounds per capita—and "the new ranching," as it is practiced today in the Texas Panhandle and across a good part of the Western plains, supports and speculates on their enormous appetite. It will probably go on supporting that appetite until no one can afford the cost, in dollars and in lost protein, of the seven or eight pounds of grain that a steer consumes to put on one pound of weight in a feed-yard pen. The economics of feeding cattle is simple. A weaned calf grows steadily and naturally on grass, but a seven-hundred-pound yearling grazing through a dry-grass season with the help of a little daily protein supplement does well simply to maintain the weight it has. It would take two more years of grazing under the best conditions to bring that yearling's weight up to the thousand and fifty or eleven hundred pounds that packers claim is the right weight, in terms of efficient family cuts, for slaughtering. And during those years that steer would be taking up valuable range space from a younger, faster-growing animal—and yielding in the end the dry, sinewy beef that cowboys like but almost no one else wants to eat. Farmers have always fed grain to their cattle—at least in winter. Ranchers have been feeding grain to steers for rapid gain and rich, tender beef ever since the range was fenced and they could no longer drive their herds north summers, following the grass season across a thousand miles. Twenty years ago—when Panhandle ranching was entirely cow-calf ranching, and no one had even thought of using his ranch as a way station for Okie calves en route to a feedyard—ranchers were shipping their steers to be fed in yards in Colorado and Arizona and California, or consigning them to stock farmers in Kansas, Illinois, Iowa, and Nebraska, to be fed with the farmers' own corn and silage. But twenty years ago people ate far less beef than they do now. Feed grains were plentiful and cheap then, and so was oil for the tractor fuel and the fertilizers a farmer needed to produce that grain.

Corn and milo, or grain sorghum, are the principal feed grains for cattle in this country, and the Panhandle—especially the southwest quadrant of the Panhandle, where the region's biggest irrigated farms are—has the capacity for producing enough corn and milo to feed all the cattle in Texas feedyards and in a good part of the Southwest, too. But as late as 1950 more than half the Panhandle was still in grass, and the bulk of the farming in the rest of it was dry-land farming. A lot of Panhandle farmers come from German peasant stock. They are not much given to changes. Some of them got rich farming long before the fifties, and when they did they used their money the way they knew a rich German farmer should. They made their yearly *Wurstfeste* bigger and beerier. They bought onto the boards of local banks and had their checkbooks printed up in German, and saved what inventiveness they had for their old feuds with local cowmen. They had problems with water, of course. The Panhandle is semiarid land. It sits on the eastern edge of the southern High Plains Terrace of the Great Plains, and it depends for water on a geological formation, the Ogallala Formation, that runs from Midland, Texas, north through Oklahoma and Kansas and well into Nebraska—a vast, isolated system cut off from any underground percolation or recharge, and potentially exhaustible. The Panhandle farmers used water where and when they found it. They had always planted some milo, but they hadn't seen much reason to dig for the water they would need for full-scale cultivation until the cattle entrepreneurs in Colorado, Arizona, and California began to promote their feedyard operations after the Second World War. There were only thirty-five hundred irrigation wells in the Panhandle in 1945. Five years later, there were fifteen thousand—and Panhandle people were talking about an agricultural production capacity that, in terms of yield and crop variety, could turn the Panhandle into as rich a farming pocket as any of California's famous valleys. After that, every farmer with the cash or the credit began irrigating. By 1960, there were nearly fifty thousand wells in the Panhandle, and the Ogallala water table was dropping two feet every year. While the local ranchers complained about the depletion of the region's water—the Panhandle gets anywhere from fifteen to twenty-three inches of rain a year, but the recharge to the Ogallala is rarely more than one inch —the farmers bought up all the land they could get hold of, put down milo, and began selling it to the same feedyards in California and the Southwest that those ranchers used for fattening their steers.

Eventually, of course, someone began to reflect on the fact that Panhandle ranchers were shipping their cattle one or two thousand miles to feed on grain that was grown a few miles from their own pastures—and to come to the conclusion that it would be cheaper and more efficient to feed those cattle at home. The man was Paul Engler. He came to Hereford, Texas, from the Middle West in 1961, and, to everyone's astonishment, he built a feedyard in that little town with space and service for five thousand animals. His sales talk was simple. Cattle that would drop fifty, or even seventy, precious pounds apiece on trucks to feedyards in, say, California could make the short trip to Hereford, in the southwest Panhandle, with no more than the normal loading-and-unloading-stress loss of three per cent—which meant fifteen pounds for a five-hundred-pound heifer and twenty for a seven-hundred-pound steer. The ranchers who listened to Engler and put their beef cattle in his new feedyard made a lot of money in 1961. They saved the cost of those extra pounds of weight loss. They saved the cost of long-distance trucking. And, paying for the same grain, they saved the grain-freight charges that were always figured into the price of feed in Arizona and California yards.

65

Within a year, the Panhandle was in the feedyard business. The president of the First National Bank of Hereford started financing feedyards, along with the purchase of cattle for those yards, and when his bank ran out of finance capital he used his own money. Then ranchers began to invest in yards, and so did corporations that owned ranches, and so did farmers and packers, until finally everyone around with a little money put aside was buying shares. By 1970, there were enough feedyards in the Panhandle to accommodate a million cattle at any one time. Given the normal four-month turnover in a yard, that meant as many as three million head a year, and, in fact, within two years' time more cattle were on feed in the Panhandle than anywhere else in the United States. Most of the important packing companies had opened slaughterhouses near the yards by then. Swift came first, with a plant just across the border in New Mexico. Then Missouri Beef arrived, and Wilson, Armour, American Beef, and Iowa Beef Processors. The local slaughterers, who in the past had always lived on orders from a few private clients, had made their own money in the boom. And so had the cattle traders and the futures speculators who moved in after 1964, when cattle became the country's newest futures commodity. In 1969, Neal B. Scott, Commodities, had opened an office at the Amarillo Livestock Auction, right across the hall from the auction ring, and now people hedged on cattle futures to the sound of pounding hooves and mooing and the ululations of the auctioneer. They touted cattle-connected stocks as the growth stocks of the decade. They bought and sold yearlings for short-term profit and prowled the yards testing feed and fretting about their animals' health and moods. One doctor, who made and lost a fortune trading futures, became a kind of local attraction as he crawled around the yard where his cattle fed, wearing his best suit and delicately probing with an outsize cattle thermometer.

The business of mixing feed was now a big business. Cattle need twenty-two or twenty-three pounds of feed a day to gain the seventy-five pounds a month that ranchers expect from a feedyard, and the feedyard rule was that anything supplying the right percentage of protein, carbohydrates, and roughage would do. Feedyards hired consultants to mix the cheapest and most efficient feed for them, and the consultants came up with formulas that involved not just milo but cottonseed hulls, dehydrated alfalfa, hay, silage, molasses, vitamins, and protein supplements—all of them spiked with the hormone diethylstilbestrol, or DES, which, at a cost to the yards of fifty or sixty cents a head, increased the conversion rate of grain to gain by ten per cent. When DES, which is a known carcinogen, got what Panhandle cattlemen prefer to describe as "a little bad publicity"—the Food and Drug Administration banned its use in feed for eighteen months because traces of the hormone started showing up in beef liver—the consultants switched to other chemicals and hormones. The new hormones, like Synovex, cost as much as a dollar a head for that ten per cent, but they managed to satisfy the F.D.A.—and F.D.A. bans are rarely generic anyway, and usually cover only the specific compounds that are named in lawsuits. The men who mixed the feeds and satisfied the F.D.A. got rich. One Phoenix nutritionist named Eugene Erwin—cattlemen call him Doc—started experimenting with alternative feeds and ended up making a thousand dollars a month, plus expenses, from thirty feed-yards that wanted his formula.

Old ranchers like to say that everyone cashed in on the Panhandle cattle boom of the nineteen-sixties and early seventies except the people who wanted to run a herd of cows as God intended. One mama cow with a nursing calf needs as much as thirty acres of grass to get along well in the Texas Panhandle. She needs those acres during two hundred and eighty-three days of gestation, too, and once her calf is weaned it needs ten or twelve acres more to sustain it through its first summer, and a costly patch of winter wheat for its first winter's grazing. By the time that calf goes on feed, at anywhere from fourteen to eighteen months, it has cost a lot in land and proper care and food supplements. In a good year, a small rancher—in the Panhandle a small rancher is someone with, say, half a million dollars' worth of land and another half a million dollars in cattle—can expect to net a profit of twenty-five to fifty thousand dollars. In a bad year, he can expect losses. Ranchers are notorious for their tax gimmickry—and there seems to be enough confusion in the statutes that cover cattle raising for ranchers' lawyers and accountants to make it a rule of thumb to claim whatever deductions look good and wait for challenges. A rancher depreciates his herds. He makes capital-gains declarations on the sale of breeder stock. He incorporates, leasing his working operation in effect to himself and deducting the cost of the lease and its entail-ments as an across-the-board business expense. And he used to be able to carry forward income that he spent on feed one year into his next year's declaration, and then his next, until that income was captured. But in a bad year, now as much as when Abel Blanton owned his six sections, no tax shelter is apt to save him if a herd of cows is all he has.

By the nineteen-sixties, private cow-calf ranching was already a luxury for rich widows and investment bankers and oil millionaires. With mass feeding and a futures market, it quickly became a symbol of what passes in Texas for old money. Ranchers who ran only cow herds and the yearlings from those cows were regarded with a kind of patronizing pride by the people who were busy making money out of cattle. They were the local Cabots and Lodges, the closest thing the Panhandle had to an aristocracy—people who could afford the wholesome pleasures of a world where sleek, fat cows sunned by water holes, handsome bulls stalked their pastures, and wobbly baby calves with loving eyes suckled beside winding paths while tall white windmills turned together in a spring breeze. They could also afford a long view of the cattle business, knowing that speculators' markets come and go but that a pampered cow produces a calf a year every year of her maturity. Still, the cattle market of the sixties and the early seventies *was* a speculators' market. It depended on high turnover in the feedyards, and it was made by risk capital and the promise of quick and often extravagant profits for as long as people kept on buying as much meat as the butcher offered and demanding more.

In that kind of market, it was the long view of the cow-calf people that began to look romantic and emotional. The same thirty acres that one mama cow used for grazing could support three yearlings fattening for the feedyard. Pastureland itself was getting scarce. In 1962, with less of the Panhandle under cultivation, most of the farmers did their planting south of the Canadian River, where the water table was often as much as a hundred feet higher than anywhere in the north. But ten years later every acre of arable land with ground water south *and* north of the breaks was in use as farmland. Farmers were taking so much Ogallala water for irrigation—and the drawdown was so severe—that in some northern counties ranchers who had always hit water at around three hundred feet had to abandon old wells and dig as deep as four hundred. Speculators had leased whatever grazing land they could get, in section parcels, and were running yearlings from the apparently inexhaustible barns of the American Southeast. And when any good grassland did come on the market, people were paying a hundred dollars an acre for it—two hundred dollars if the land had access to a paved road.

Some ranchers began to take back land they had been leasing for years to smaller ranchers—Panhandle grass leases, by tradition, last a year and have to be renewed—and that way kept their cows and calves and still had land to spare for running extra yearlings. Some moved their cows to places like New Mexico, where the grazing ratio was forty-five acres to a cow, but where the land, being nearly bone-dry, rarely sold for more than fifty dollars an acre. They saved their Texas grass for their own weaned calves and whatever others they might want to buy. Some ranchers sold all their cows and bulls and converted their operations entirely. Some cut their herds by half—running Southern yearlings for quick profit but keeping enough mama cows for their own security, the way an investor might balance a portfolio between new growth stocks and comfortable blue chips with a steady yield. Henry's rancher diversified. He speculated on feedyards, put in winter wheat, traded fodder feed, and hedged the cattle futures. But he kept his twenty-two hundred mama cows, and in 1968 he cancelled enough leases to be able to run a few thousand extra yearlings at any one time, and even keep them on wheat for six months of the year.

Cowboys call yearling ranches "calf hotels," because calves use them like hotels—stopping on their way from a farm to a feedyard for a little grazing, a little fresh air and medicine, and the ministrations of an able staff. It was never difficult to fill those hotels. More cattle were raised in Texas itself than in any other state, and tens of thousands of small farmers in the Southeast owned a couple of milk cows that always managed to produce a calf a year—if not by plan, then by chance encounters with the local bulls. The farmers had always kept those calves to eat themselves, or had sold them, cheap, to neighbors at their country auctions. Now, gradually, their auction barns filled up with ranchers' agents, who bought whatever they could get, bidding up the price of scrawny calves just off their mothers' milk to far more than anyone had ever paid before. The farmers supplying calves to Panhandle ranches were mainly poor dirt farmers. The new market in Okie calves gave most of them the first real money they had ever made in livestock, and they responded to the windfall by letting their cows breed, so the saying went, with "anything on four legs that snorts." By the early seventies, ranchers were paying up to eighty cents a pound, price on delivery, for a three-hundred-pound Okie calf—the price is half that now—and still, with good grazing and the right feed, making a considerable profit when that calf went to the packers at eleven hundred pounds for an on-the-hoof price per pound of forty or fifty cents.

Given the proper care, a young calf recovered easily from underfeeding at home and the weight loss of a long truck ride. It fattened quickly on Texas grass into a reasonably respectable animal—and at not much cost to the rancher who had bought it. Ranchers figured their expenses on a weaned calf or a yearling at about four dollars a month during the grass season, which ran from around April through October—April Fools' Day to Halloween was the rule of thumb. During the winter-wheat season, they expected a yearling to put on a pound and a half a day, at a cost to the rancher of twenty cents for every pound of gain. In a year of good weather and sufficient gain, the formula was nearly foolproof. But the yearling men, caught up in their success, began to tout their Okie cattle—products of the most random, unscientific breeding the business had ever seen—for hybrid vigor. Ranchers who had always thought of hybrid vigor as something that happened when they put a prize Angus bull on a prize Hereford heifer to produce a prime-quality Black Baldy calf, were talking suddenly about Okie hardiness. They began to lobby the Department of Agriculture for changes in the beef-grading regulations that would acknowledge their investment. They had to fight the packers, who had their own lobby, for those changes, but eventually they won, and the result was that the categories—prime, choice, good, and standard—and, consequently, the prices for inspected beef were altered to reflect not only the traditional quality grading but also yield grading, which has to do with the proportion of marketable meat on a carcass.

The yearling boom was a ten-year wonder. By the end of 1972, some sixty-five per cent of the Panhandle's grass was given over entirely to yearling ranching. The Panhandle was producing only about twenty per cent of the state's cattle by then, but at one time or another that year eighty-five per cent of all the beef cattle in Texas had fed, if not grazed, within a hundred and fifty miles of Amarillo. In fact, when the oil crisis hit the country over the next year, more cattle were on feed in the Texas Panhandle than anywhere else in the country. And a lot of the people who owned those cattle lost their money trying to keep them there. There was a certain frontier irony in the fact that it was cattlemen who went bankrupt keeping up with the price of farmers' grain, but not even the farmers were much comforted. The farmers depended on oil for their harvesters and tractors and for the power to make their irrigation systems function. They depended on petroleum-based sprays and fertilizers, and in 1973 they were paying three hundred dollars for a ton of fertilizer that had cost them sixty dollars in 1972. To make a profit, they needed to pass those costs along—at least as much of them as the market would tolerate. Russia, buying up the subsidized reserves in corn and wheat, left the country with such a scarcity of grain that year that cattlemen, in fact, were forced to pay whatever the farmers asked for milo. And milo itself was in short supply by 1974, when the harvest yield in Texas alone fell a hundred million bushels short of the yield the year before. A hundred pounds of milo went for two dollars and fourteen cents before the oil crisis and the deal that Texas cattlemen refer to as the Russian grain drain. Two years later, the price was over six dollars, and for the cattlemen that meant the cost per pound of grain in a feedyard, which had run about thirty cents before the crisis, went up to sixty cents, and even eighty cents, at a time when cattle were selling for only thirty-seven cents a pound.

Ranchers like to say that in the cattle business your first loss is always your best loss, but no one seems to have considered that in the panic of a collapsing market. A lot of people held their steers on feed, expecting the government to act to save them. They held their steers on feed during the housewives' boycott in the spring of 1973 and during the beef-price freeze that summer, knowing that the freeze was ending in September. They held them on feed through a truckers' strike that fall and on into the winter—all of them still waiting to be saved. By the end of the year, most of the steers in Panhandle feedyards had long since passed the weight at which eight pounds of feed stood them to a pound of gain. They were eating twelve to fifteen pounds of feed for every pound they gained. They were "overdone," as people say in the cattle business. At upward of twelve hundred and fifty pounds a head, they were too big and too fatty for efficient cuts, and their two hundred pounds of extra weight—the invisible animal, ranchers call it—was practically worthless. When the cattlemen finally tried to sell their steers at the packinghouses, there was a glut on the market, and a lot of them ended up taking losses of over two hundred dollars a head on animals they could have unloaded six months earlier at a loss of only twenty or thirty dollars.

It took a year longer before the cattle market began to turn. The oilmen and the bankers, the corporate presidents and the rich widows survived that year, but everybody else with money in beef cattle lost more of it than he could even begin to recover with a clever tax form. A lot of the Panhandle's feedyards closed that year, too. Ranchers, trying to recoup, were buying fewer calves and grazing the ones they had longer, and the feedyards that stayed in business were rarely more than a quarter full. Paul Engler's old feedyard —the one that began the cattle boom in west Texas and grew to accommodate fifty thousand head of cattle—never had more than eighteen thousand animals on feed in the spring of 1975, and, even so, the yard's new owners considered themselves lucky.

Everyone blamed everyone else for the crisis. The packers blamed the supermarkets, which they claimed had hoarded beef to keep the prices up and had consequently stopped reordering. American Beef, one of the biggest packers in the country, had bought up twenty-five million dollars' worth of beef for its slaughterhouses—beef that it couldn't pay for—and then had to petition for reorganization under the bankruptcy law. The cattlemen blamed the packers, who in trying to cut their own losses had virtually stopped buying any more cattle. The farmers blamed the ranchers for not supporting the feed-grain business they had helped create. They all blamed the government for ignoring their various demands for help. And while they were busy blaming and defending, the cattle business slowly started to recover.

By the spring of 1975 the price of milo had dropped to four dollars and fifty cents a hundred pounds. The feedyards accordingly dropped their prices, so that the cost per pound of grain to a rancher went down to around forty-five cents again. When a cattle feeder from California, who

Panhandle people said was buying for the Shah of Iran, placed bids on nearly half the cattle that passed through the Amarillo Livestock Auction that spring—after he had already bought tens of thousands of head of Panhandle cattle and shipped them to the Coast to feed—the encouraging rumor went around that rich Middle Easterners would pay good money for just about any animal that ate grass. Panhandle ranchers sent their agents south again and cautiously began to buy more Okies. But what saved the ranchers in the end was that people had simply got used to the inflation. Americans were making a consummately American decision to pay more money for their beef rather than do without it. They started buying, and eventually they bought more of it than they ever had, because the price of everything else was up so much that no one saved enough eating chicken or pork chops instead of hamburger, or even steak, to make a difference.

By now, Panhandle ranchers have begun to treat their cattle crash as a kind of object lesson in frontier history. They say that they were a little too enthusiastic, perhaps, a little too greedy and "unscientific" in their judgments, but those ten bonanza years on the Texas Panhandle have changed the style of ranching there as irrevocably as railroad boxcars and barbed wire did a hundred years ago. There are parts of America where ranching has kept its character. Up in Montana, the ranchers still run herds of their favorite cows, and their cows calve every spring, and their yearlings pasture in the summer on mountains that the state preserves as open range. But the Panhandle is not one of those places. West Texans live on the frontier of money. They believe in luck and high stakes and big killings

76

—in oil splashing up suddenly from a neighbor's pasture, in feedyards that in ten years' time are servicing a million steers. Panhandle ranchers are still running other people's yearlings, and they are waiting for the next windfall. There are more yearlings fattening on Panhandle grass today than there ever were. Memory is short in west Texas, and only the cowboys and the rich widows talk much anymore about the good old days of ranching.

Chapter 8

ONE Sunday, early in May, Henry Blanton hitched his horse trailer to his pickup truck, and he and Betsy drove down toward Canadian to pay a call on their friends George and Emily Smith. Henry admired George Smith more than any other man he knew. He liked to say that George had come up in the world the right way —starting as a cowboy, working hard and saving money and, finally, leasing some land, one section at a time, and filling that land with a fine small herd of cattle. George was in his seventies now, and so was Emily, but they ran their spread themselves, without a hand to help them. Most mornings at six-thirty, they saddled their horses and rode out to check their cows and their fences—George with a day's supply of cigarillos in the pocket of his denim jacket, and Emily with her long, platinumed hair pulled back under the silk scarf with the golden bridle printed on it that she had discovered in the window of Hermès on her big fiftieth-anniversary trip to Paris.

Cowboys driving the highway that bordered the Smiths' pastures kept an eye out for George and Emily, and they always stopped to neighbor if the Smiths needed help. They took a personal interest in the Smiths' fortunes, because the Smiths were, as the cowboys put it, "one of ours." In fact, the Smiths were the only people a lot of Panhandle cowboys knew who had started off poor—as poor as they themselves were now—and made a success as ranchers without so much as a small oil well to tide them over in bad times. George and Emily, in their fifty years together, had survived the Depression, the dust bowl, another long drought, and two tornadoes that carried off their house and barn and killed their horses. They had lost the lease on their last ranch in 1969, when the man who owned the land started running yearlings, and that night they had broken out a bottle of champagne and toasted the future of their next one. Emily had sold her diamond-horseshoe earrings to pay for the sections they owned now, but, as she always said, no cattle she was likely to come across were going to know the difference between a diamond and a hunk of glass. She and George never went to the country club, where the women needed their diamonds for sitting by the pool on Sunday afternoons while their husbands played golf. George and Emily preferred the company of cowboys. Every Saturday night, George put on his fancy boots and a handmade Western shirt while Emily smudged her eyelids with bright-blue shadow, painted her mouth with Christian Dior No. 59, and hung her new rhinestone horseshoes from her freshly rouged ears, and then the two of them drove to the country-and-Western dance in Pampa, with enough bourbon in the trunk of their Continental for every thirsty cowboy at their table. Sunday mornings, they slept late and drank a lot of black coffee. By noon, Emily had usually set out a new bottle, a pitcher of iced tea, and a plate of Oreo cookies on the kitchen table and was ready for Sunday company. This Sunday, though, she and George had work. Their cows were calving. Some had already dropped their calves and were off grazing, but the pasture near the house was still full of huge, logy cows waiting to deliver, and George and Emily were busy sorting out the heifers due for their first babies. They intended to move them to a little calving pasture by the barn, where they could look after them and help them, because a delicate Hereford heifer bred to a big Brangus bull often had a hard time calving. Some years, only a few heifers suffered. But there were years when George spent half the spring pulling calves from their mothers, and so the Smiths liked to keep their heifers by the barn, where George stored the ratchet and ropes and pulling chains he used in an emergency.

It was Betsy who spotted Emily in a far corner of the pasture. Emily was running her paint, Diamond Lil, in fast, narrowing circles around a fat heifer, slapping her thigh and yelling "Ho hey!" while her Paris scarf flapped in the wind and her cigarillo bobbed up and down on her wet red lipstick. George, across the pasture on his bay, Rusty, was minding the gate to a roomy pen that already held some twenty heifers. He waved a stick at Emily when she rode toward him, driving in her heifer, and then he flicked the

80

stick, beat the animal into the pen, and shut the gate behind it.

Henry led his black Appaloosa, Pepper, out of the trailer and rode back out with Emily. She had been having trouble all morning with one skittish heifer that even now, as they galloped toward it, ducked past them and burrowed into the protective jumble of the cows. Henry started circling in on it, slowly and precisely, and he kept on circling, cutting the herd back with every pass, until most of the cows had scattered and his heifer stood out, trembling and vulnerable.

"Pretty work! Pretty work!" George called, pointing his stick at Henry.

Betsy, who had climbed onto a rail of the pen to watch, nodded. People enjoyed seeing Henry work with Pepper. He was at his best on the Appaloosa. There was something comfortable and generous about the way they accommodated to each other—something that made Betsy a little sad, because she saw it, with Henry, so rarely lately. Henry had bought the Appaloosa as a colt from a trader he liked in Perryton. He had broken him at two and a half, and trained him every day over the next year, until the horse was ready for his first roundup. Pepper was nine now. He was a big horse—nearly sixteen hands—but he was gentle and fast and accurate, and these days he was the only horse on the Willow Ranch that seemed to command Henry's tenderness and humor. No one else was allowed to ride Pepper, and by now he and Henry worked cattle with a rhythm all their own. Betsy hardly noticed Henry shift his weight a few inches in the saddle, but Pepper spun sharply, and in a moment the heifer blinked and looked around to discover herself alone in a stretch of pasture. After that, she came in calmly.

"Right pretty work," George said again.

Emily puffed on her cigarillo. "That was one jittery heifer," she said.

Henry grinned. He was flushed and feeling easy and accomplished.

"Old Em got the hard job this morning, seeing as it's me with the worst hangover," George said, riding into the pen with the heifer, which promptly began to bang a flank against the rails, lowing. "Just look at that silly old thing," George said. "She can't hardly move none, and she can't hardly stand still, neither."

"She's all floppy behind," Emily said fondly.

"She's fixing to have that baby any minute now," Betsy said.

Emily sighed loudly. "This sorting sure is hard. You have to round them in, and half the time they get away and you're back where you started." She leaned forward and rubbed her horse behind the ears while Betsy rummaged in her pocketbook for some sugar cubes. "I bet you're sweating, honey," Emily crooned to Diamond Lil. "That little old horned heifer, she sure got us up."

"Well, never mind. We'll have a pasture full of little old calves soon," George said, squinting out across the pasture. And then, to Henry and Betsy, "You know that there farmer that showed up at the dance last night? Well, it weren't more than seven this morning when the phone rings, and it's that old farmer, wanting to know if—"

"Like near scared me to death, hearing the phone ring that early on a Sunday morning," Emily said, producing a flask of bourbon from her saddlebag. Emily had the prerogatives of age and a lusty character, and used them. She drank with the men and cursed better than most of them, and she often said that she had kept George home nights for fifty years by providing the proper fuel and the proper company in his own kitchen. Even Betsy felt obliged to take a sip of bourbon when Emily passed a bottle.

"Hush, Em," George said. "I'm telling this." He winked at Betsy, who was feeding a sugar cube to Rusty now. "Em is a little set up today, 'cause I danced with so many pretty girls last night. But I told her, 'Em, honey, it's you I always go home with and—' "

Henry blushed, and Betsy looked horrified.

"Now where was I?" George said, puzzled. "Right. This here farmer's on the telephone, and he's saying that since we all got on so well together last night, maybe I could do him a little favor and say if there's some old cowpuncher I know who'd like to make himself a little money helping this here farmer that's short of hands with his plowing."

"They sure are very different, farmers are," Henry said, shaking his head.

"That's what I told him," George replied. "I told him, 'Now, you don't want to insult nobody, do you, paying for a little help.' I said that cowmen, like me and Em—why, if we're fixing to brand we just notify our friends. The way *we* live, it's just people helping people. It's people neighboring. Like when a cowman has a grass fire, I says, why you just get everybody out there helping. Whereas I heard for a fact, I says—but polite-like—that when certain farmers have a fire they have to go and call the firemen."

"They sure ain't independent—that's one thing," Henry

said. "They got to have them co-ops, just to be sure no one's taking advantage of them. They got to have everything written down before they do for each other."

"Well, they do dance pretty," Emily said. "That sure was a bunch of them last night."

"*I* wouldn't sit down with none of them," Henry told her. "I got a lot of kinfolk is farmers, but I don't approve of them. You take a farmer—he's pumping five hundred gallons of water a minute. That's water that belongs to all of us. But if one of your cows gets on his land he'll start cussing, or if he's educated some he'll sue you. One of them pulled a gun on me last week when all I was doing was going down this road of his looking for a cow. Boy, I sure got mad. I said that to me the law always was that if a man wants to keep my cows out it's up to him to do it. Hell, farmers was the ones who fenced this country up in the first place. Anyhow, he got real mad and said he wants me to sign this piece of paper saying I'm responsible for any of my cows that get onto his land."

"Imagine," Betsy said. "I guess it's that farmers, they live in a different world. Ten miles—it could just as well be ten thousand. And they're not around each other much, the way cowboys are, so they don't know much about getting along with people."

George waited for a minute and said to Henry, "I sure do hope you and Lester Hill got something down on paper about that deal of yours."

Henry looked at the sky, embarrassed.

"That's what I keep telling Henry—sign something," Betsy said quietly. "It seems to me he ought to be a little cautious, seeing as how Lester is always taking advantage

84

of him. I mean, the phone's always ringing, or that radio gadget in the truck, and there's Lester saying, 'Henry, do this, do that.' And it's not ranch work. It's Lester wanting someone to help him clean his swimming pool, or fix his roof, or run over to the feedyard and make sure those Okie calves he keeps trading on the side are getting the right feed."

Henry glared at her. "Seems to me a man's handshake ought to be enough. My Granddaddy Abel never signed no contract. My granddaddy always said a man's word should be his contract, and that's what I do believe, and that's what any cowboy believes, and"—he took a long drink—"that's how I'm going to live."

"Your granddaddy couldn't write," Betsy said. "Those old cowpunchers—they shook hands so as not to embarrass each other."

"Well, at least your granddaddy knew this place when it was cow-calf country," George said. "Before them yearling people discovered what stout short grass we got here." George shook his head. "I ain't meaning you, Henry—I mean about them yearling fellows. I know you hate those Okies as much as me and Em here. And a man's got to start somewhere."

Henry was thinking. "One thing's true, people sure is jealous of Texas grass," he said at last. "Remember when they had those caterpillars over in New Mexico? They wanted to spray, and we stopped them, 'cause one rain and that spray would come all the way on over here, polluting the reservoir down at Lake Meredith, polluting all our water. Boy, they sure was mad at Texas, I know. I was visiting in New Mexico then, and you could hear those caterpillars. They came in a line. On a clear day, you could hear them eating up that poor old Mexico grass, and—" Henry stopped himself. "You know, it used to make me bitter, not having my own ranch. Guess I always thought I would, someday." He leaned over and took an Oreo cookie from Emily's saddlebag. "I'll tell you what makes me bitter now—it's the ones who inherit, or the ones who come in with so much money and can't do what I do." Henry laughed. "Course, sometimes I think that if that old lake got polluted and had to be drained away, things might be a whole lot better. I mean, a lot of people would leave, and it'd be a real nice place again."

Emily looked cross. "It's their place—those people—as well as yours, Henry."

Henry shook his head. "It's getting to be like New York City around here. You know, I heard on television there's a million people on welfare in New York City. It's 'cause they got a bad system. Now, you study ants, that's got this real good system worked out, and you see why—"

"You can't go back, Henry," George said. "What if you was still having to go round in a wagon?"

Henry told George that he had a cousin who preferred wagons, a cousin who had stood at the gate to his land with a shotgun when the town came in with orders to lay a paved road.

"Henry, we never had a toilet in our lives till we built this house," Emily said. "Hell, 1947 was my first bathtub. First hot water, too. And I'll tell you something. I like it, on a cold night, just when I'm getting to sleep, not having to go clear across the yard and—"

86

"We're all for modern times, me and Em," George put in. "You young ones never lived way back, jumping up in the middle of the night, with no lights, trying to find that old outhouse."

"I sure did," Henry said, fingering a cigarette. "Till I was five or six, anyhow. We had no electricity, no plumbing, no heat, no running water. And I did it again when I started cowboying. Least, I did till I got this job. And it weren't so bad"—Henry grinned suddenly—"though I never did know why they always put the outhouse way back behind the woodshed. To be inconvenient—that's all I can figure."

"Why, even here we didn't have a phone at first," Betsy said. "We been on six ranches since Henry started cowboying, and this is the first that's had any conveniences. There was one with no water for my washing machine. We had this pump in the well, but it didn't work, and I had to get my water from a creek. Had to carry it in buckets up a real steep hill."

Henry chuckled. "One day, Betsy here was packing those two buckets up the hill, and her mother and daddy showed up visiting. Well, her mother fell to crying. She said she never did think she'd have to see her daughter doing that, same as she used to."

"And *I* said, 'Mama, if Henry wanted to go to Africa and live in a mud hut, I'd go with him.'" Betsy looked at Henry shyly. She had taken a drink, and bourbon made her sentimental. "I think back on those days, and I think that must have been the happiest time of my life."

Henry took the flask from her. "People knew how to do for themselves then. Nowadays, a kid gets scratched and it's right to the doctor. Now, when I was a kid it was kerosene and chewing tobacco."

Emily said that her mother had used kerosene for coughs —kerosene with a little sugar. And Betsy said that hers had mixed whiskey and rock candy when the children had a fever. Then Henry claimed he could remember the day he heard a radio for the first time.

George guffawed. "Henry, I *know* they had radios when you was little."

Henry shook his head, stubborn.

"Come on, Henry. Don't you tell me about those old days. I was in them. And don't tell me about those antiques, either, 'cause I lived with them."

"Well, there *was* a hell of a lot more family life then," Emily said, musing. She leaned down and patted Betsy on the arm. "Course, there weren't no conveyances to get you away from your family."

"Didn't you think people was better then?" Henry asked her.

George chuckled. "We never did get to see no people to find out. If there was a dance, it was once a month and you stayed two days." He squinted at Henry. "And when you did see someone, you was right proud."

"Then I just can't understand why you keep talking about liking progress," Henry said. "Progress *is* conveyances. It's old Ed Loomis cutting up and down some highway. That's progress. It's them farmers making seventy-five thousand dollars a year from the government for not growing anything. And a town where there's no more country-thinking people, and juries where they'll believe anything a nigger tells them, and all them long-hair feedyard hippies."

"Buffalo Bill and them Indians—they didn't go near no barber, either, and I don't hear you taking on against them," George said. George liked Henry, and worried a lot about him.

"Did your daddy have a mustache?" Henry asked.

"Yup."

"You see," Henry said. "Your daddy had a mustache, but you wouldn't ever wear one."

Emily tucked a strand of platinum hair back under her Paris scarf. "I remember when they let me bob my hair," she told Betsy. "Why, my daddy went round that pasture and like near cried. He said, 'Sweet babe, you don't look like yourself no more.' "

"Was it feedyard hippies you and Tom met in the package store the other week?" George said. "Seems like I heard something about that."

Betsy said, "Oh, Henry."

"You and Tom up to more mischief?" Emily said. "I swear, I don't know who's leading who astray. Like the time you and Tom roped that stray and hailed that poor old doctor in his car and talked him up about giving him that steer. Shoot, you had that poor old doctor believing he could drive right off with that old steer sitting like a baby in the back seat. Now, don't you deny it, Henry. I heard that old doctor like near died, trying to drive with that mean old steer hanging around his neck and bellowing like crazy and—"

"They called us goddam hats," Henry lied, and he immediately looked cheerful. "You should of seen Tom. He took to beating up on both them hippies just as they was taking off. And all the time he's shouting about how they owed him an apology."

George slapped his knee, laughing.

"Henry!" Betsy said.

"Well, Betsy, you got to be always ready to defend yourself," Henry said. "You know, I always figured a true cowboy was a little like a coyote. I mean, he won't bother you at all till you get him cornered."

Betsy turned away.

"If you was the sheriff, you would of said to shoot them hippies dead and lay a stick on them," Henry told her. "Truly. There was this one time I heard the sheriff say if you catch a man stealing your cattle or fixing to fight you, don't arrest him and turn him in, and, whatever you do, don't wound him. Otherwise, he'll be after you with his gun or his lawyers. Best thing to do, the sheriff said, is to shoot him dead, where he can't touch you." Henry shifted, uneasy, in his saddle. "Well, that's what they always did when there was just cattlemen out here."

Betsy tried to smile. "Come on, now, Henry, you know you wouldn't kill no one." She looked at Emily, pleading. "Why, if Henry has a cow or a horse that needs killing, he goes and gets one of the hands to do it for him. And there was that day Henry gave a lift to two hippies. Brought them home to lunch, even—he felt so sorry for them. And once he gave this old nigger on the road five dollars, and when the girls asked him why he done it he said it was 'cause the nigger was sick and broke. He said he'd have done the same for a stray dog. Henry just likes to joke some, and . . ."

90

Then, to Henry, "It was raining that day. You know I always worry on a rainy day. The cowboys start drinking early and . . . Oh, Henry, what good does it do you?"

Henry leaned across his horse toward her. "I was protecting your interests, Betsy. Yours and mine."

Chapter 9

HENRY was six years old when his family got together to see about a horse and the right gear for
him. That was one of the responsibilities a boy's
family had then, along with a hot meal once a day and shoes
for school. It did not much matter if the boy lived on a
ranch or had moved to town with his mother, the way
Henry had in 1942, when the Army took his father. Panhandle towns were tiny in those days—a few houses, a store,
and perhaps a post office. Most houses opened at the back
on pastures, and even the smallest and shabbiest of them
came with a provision barn, or, at least, a shed where a
horse could winter. Henry's horse shared his shed with
sacks of flour and potatoes and onions. At the time that
Abel Blanton bought the horse, the horse was called Pal,

but when he started nibbling through the sacks in the shed Henry renamed him Onion. Onion was a problem—"not what you would call a real good kind of horse," Henry always said when he was reminiscing. Onion was ornery and bucked a lot and enjoyed kicking over the chair that Henry, at six, climbed to mount him. It took a while for them to arrive at the abusive, affectionate arrangement that Henry later claimed was so instructive to them both.

Henry broke Onion to a big used saddle with a mended horn, which his Granddaddy Wesley—his mother's father—contributed, and to a bridle that came by way of his father's oldest brother. There were Blanton brothers all over Texas by that time. Abel Blanton was a lusty man, for all his hell-fire sermonizing. He had ridden home from every one of his long spring roundups with the intention of leaving Mrs. Blanton pregnant when he rode out again, and for years, more often than not, he did. Ten children survived, and seven of them were boys, and they all cowboyed —except one who roughnecked in the oil fields near Houston and one who took up pentecostalism and died from shock, caressing a prairie rattler at a revival meeting back east in Tennessee.

Henry's father, whose name was James Jonah Blanton, left school at sixteen for a job at one of the big Panhandle ranches. At seventeen, he was courting Amy MacLeod, the foreman's daughter, and at eighteen he married her, in spite of Abel's assurances that by marrying into Wesley MacLeod's Methodist family he was taking a long shot on his eternal life. James Jonah wanted to be a rancher. Like Abel before him, he dreamed of his own land and his own cattle, but the Depression and the dust had settled on west

Texas, and even with the money he won bulldogging and racing wild mares at cowboy rodeos, there was never anything left at the end of the month for him to put away. He had heard that people were striking gold lodes in Arizona —cowboys who had lost their jobs at home were coming back from a few months' work in Arizona gold mines and talking about heading out again to prospect on their own. When Henry was nine months old and just past colic, James Jonah sold his horse and saddle, bought three tickets for the train to Tucson, and told his wife to pack lightly, because before she knew it she would be coming home. They spent the next year and a half in Arizona, in an Army-surplus tent that James Jonah found abandoned at the edge of a mining shantytown. Amy tried to make a home of it. She laid linoleum on the ground, and James Jonah built a pine cabinet for her pots and pans. They bought a kerosene lamp for the tent, and then a chair and a baby's cot and a big iron bedstead, but after a month they moved the bed outdoors. Once, when Amy was old and sorting out her memories, she told her sons that she and their father would lie in that iron bed at night crying—looking at the stars and trying to pretend they were out on a roundup at the ranch.

It was a bad year for Amy, raising a baby in a rough settlement, caught up in the desperation of poor people who lived for the strike that only a very few of them would make. James Jonah never struck so much as a nugget. Wesley MacLeod had to take up a collection on the ranch to move the family home, and James Jonah never left the ranch again until he volunteered for the Second World War. He wanted to fight the Germans—he imagined the Germans as a whole race of homesteaders—but the Army sent him to the South Pacific, and he never forgave the Army for betraying him. Henry always said that it was missing the Germans that broke his father's spirit, as much as the Japanese shrapnel that left him lame in the right leg and ended his days as a cowboy and his future as a cowman. James Jonah Blanton came home from an Army hospital in the Marianas and never worked the range again. He repaired the pine cabinet from his Arizona tent, and—while Amy was busy teaching grade school or practicing hairdos for her beautician's license, and little Henry was matching wits with Onion in the back yard—he sat in the parlor polishing his old rodeo trophies and arranging and rearranging them on the cabinet shelves. He took a job, finally, checking stock in the warehouse of a barn-construction company, and after that he led a quiet, bitter life and laid his hopes on Henry.

James Jonah used to tell Henry that there was cowboying in the family blood. He invented glorious tall stories about Henry's Granddaddy Abel and Granddaddy Wesley, who in fact had stowed away in the bedroll wagon of a passing trail gang at the age of eleven and had never shown up again at his parents' cotton farm, down in Coleman County. But James Jonah no longer had the heart to take up Henry's education as a cowboy. His grandfathers saw to that instead. Henry worked a branding iron at the age of eight. At ten he cut his first steer, and a year later he could rope a calf by the hind legs. He rode dogies and then steers and saddle broncs. He learned how to fall, and how to take a lot of kicking, and how to walk home black and blue without crying. He was out with his cousin Petey MacLeod when Petey's horse tripped and fell and split Petey's head open.

Henry slung the dead boy over the empty saddle and, leading Petey's horse, brought him home to his mother. He was out roping with one of Abel's hands when a crazed steer dragged the hand to death. Abel, who drove his cattle like a herd of sinners and encouraged his hands to do the same, had this to say at the funeral: "Old Father Time, he'll get you in the end, and it don't matter none that you been taking precautions." But Granddaddy Wesley, whom Henry consulted, grieving, started his lessons in cowboy common sense. He taught him that a cowboy was always gentle, that the best way and the right way to ride a horse or rope a calf was the quietest way possible. He said that what made a real hand was not so much knowing how to do something as knowing when to do something—the most important "when" being when to leave an animal alone.

Wesley was a patient, humorous man, but he and Abel Blanton argued a lot over Henry's instruction—the two old cowpunchers rocking fiercely in the chairs reserved for them on the neutral ground of their children's parlor. Wesley had the authority on the ranch where he was foreman. He liked to experiment, crossbreeding cattle, whereas Abel was convinced that breeding animals was a wicked trick of the evolutionists. Abel did not want his grandson listening to nonsense about crossbreeding for a better beef stock, but breeding happened to be one of the things that troubled Henry most when he was growing up. He and his Granddaddy Wesley used to talk secretly about the problem—Henry always took his religious problems to Wesley—and eventually they managed to work it to its logical conclusion, which was that cows evolved but people were set down perfect, at the Creation, by the hand of God. That

96

was what Henry came to believe at ten, and it was what he still believed at forty, although by now he rarely went to church and knew from his girls that some teachers at the district high school had been mentioning evolution for years.

No one was allowed to mention evolution in school when Henry was a boy. There were Bible classes every day, and boys who told dirty stories about the Virgin Birth got ten strokes from the principal's horsewhip. Henry was whipped once. He came home from school with welts on his back that were far worse than any welts he ever got when his father or Abel beat him in the shed for misbehaving or sassing. His little brother Tom cried, seeing him so hurt, and got a whipping, too. That was when Henry started taking his instruction from the movies, where all the cowboys were like Abel's hands and practiced the religion of the great outdoors.

At first, Henry's Granddaddy Wesley took him to the movies. Every other Saturday—except, of course, at calving time on Wesley's ranch—they drove in Wesley's jeep a hundred and five miles to Amarillo and made the rounds of the movie theatres, watching one Western after another, with the old man poking and pointing and guffawing, and sometimes even shouting at the screen. Afterward, at the soda fountain, they went over the day's movies, one by one, discussing what was accurate and appropriate and what was not. In a few years, Tom joined them on their Saturday excursions. And then Henry and Tom started playing hooky on weekdays and hitching rides to Amarillo alone. They took up brooding like Joel McCrea. They practiced staring into sunsets. They tried on John Wayne's wise, squinty looks and Gary Cooper's virile silences. They lit campfires in the back yard and sat there after supper, alert to all sorts of danger in the darkness past the shed. They rode their horses as if rustlers were after them, or wild Indians. They longed for six-guns. They kept the girls in town giggling as they trotted down Main Street with their empty holsters, tipping big black hats to everyone they saw.

Henry had plans for the future. He was a grade-school and then a high-school hero. He won the games for the football team, and took all the track trophies home, and scored the most points in basketball. Mothers like Betsy Barton's mother made a great deal of his rosy cheeks and pale-gray eyes and the shock of sandy hair that fell across his forehead. For three straight years, he was voted the best athlete in his class and the boy most likely to succeed in life. The high-school yearbooks were full of his pictures— Henry Blanton throwing the touchdown pass, Henry Blanton shooting the winning basket, Henry Blanton raising the Confederate flag in the senior homeroom. He had given his class ring to the prettiest girl in high school—it was Tom who had pointed out that Betsy looked just like Jennifer Jones in "Duel in the Sun," only blond and, of course, white. Betsy was Homecoming Queen to Henry's King. People saw her in the paper twirling her baton in the finals of a big state twirling contest on the same day that Henry was on another page of the paper accepting a football scholarship to college. That night, Hugh Doyle, the rancher who had always hired Henry summers, paid a call on James Jonah and Amy Blanton to offer his congratulations. He said that once Henry finished college, he was going to take him on and, if things went well, help him get started on his own.

Henry had one year at a big state college before he lost his scholarship. He often thought of that year now, wondering why, suddenly, he was so ashamed of himself and so unimportant to everybody else. He had never been a stranger anywhere before except as a baby in Arizona. He did not know what to say to boys who had money for cars and whiskey and fraternities or to teachers who could look at a paper he had spent a month writing and tell him he had managed "an adequate sixth-grade theme." The girls, especially, confused him. He was never able to forget the day a girl corrected him in English class, in front of everyone —people had started laughing when he got angry and told her that, as he understood the Bible, women were supposed to listen respectfully to men, not speak out against them. That was the day he wrote home to Betsy saying that the time had come to get engaged. They were married in June, in the Baptist Church where Betsy had gone to Sunday school. And they had a fine wedding, although Henry's Granddaddy Wesley did remark several times that he would have given a lot to see old Abel Blanton, who had died at ninety, alive and kicking up a fuss about Baptists. Betsy walked down the aisle with a pouf of tulle balanced on her blond head and six bridesmaids marching solemnly before her; Henry waited at the altar, scrubbed red, half scalped by a Pampa barber, and dressed up in his going-to-college suit. That night, Henry locked himself in the bathroom of their motel room on U.S. 66, reading and rereading the instructions on a box of contraceptives, which he had no idea how to use. It was Betsy who got him out, banging on the door and saying that God would guide them, that God didn't approve of those contraptions anyway. The next morning, they went shopping in Amarillo. Betsy bought a rocking chair for her first parlor, and then Henry took her to Feferman's Western Wear and asked Abe Feferman to show him the best black rancher Stetson in the store.

Mattie Blanton was born one night the following spring while Henry was working the late shift in an east-Texas foundry. East Texas was full of little church colleges with basketball and football teams, and one of them had offered Henry another scholarship. It was Betsy who talked him into going back to school. She had never intended to have a baby then. She wanted to study home economics, and Henry was trying to make sense of a major in animal science from a Christian perspective and at the same time hold down his job at the foundry to support them both. He might have stayed in school if there had been a ranch nearby where he could have worked after classes and had the use of a free house for his new family.

"I'd wake up in the morning all tired from that foundry deal, and then I'd get to thinking about those summers cowboying," Henry said a few days after his visit to the Smiths. It was early in the morning, and he was sitting on the chuck wagon, out by the well at headquarters, watching the sky take color and waiting for his hands. "I'd think how I knew more about cows than any of them professors, and how maybe education and experience don't necessarily work together. What I mean is, if you're going to run a ranch you're going to learn how on that old ranch better than in any classroom. I'd keep on thinking all day at college. And at night, in that old foundry, where the heat was so intense, I'd be daydreaming about some pasture, and I'd come home and say to Betsy that it sure beat me if this was any way to live. Betsy, she'd get after me to stay and get me an education. But, you know, a cowboy can't stand a domineering woman. I mean, I always did look down on a woman that tried to tell a man what to do. But then Mattie got born. We didn't expect her, and Betsy cried and cried, and I got a little scared, even. But when that baby came I couldn't feel too bad about it, 'cause I never could stay studying *and* support a baby, and that kind of settled things, didn't it? The first thing I did was call up old Mr. Doyle. He had this office at the Amarillo Hotel, and I called him there and he was real disappointed—I mean about my leaving college and all that—but he was real nice about it. He said, 'You always got a job with me, Henry,' and I said, 'Sir, I'll take it now.'

"He put us in this old house on his ranch. It wasn't much —the house. It was north of the breaks, over near the New Mexico border, on some sections where he ran about a thousand head of cows winters and summered his yearlings. We was really alone there. The closest town was thirty miles, and there were no neighbors—only farmers. I mean, no one to neighbor for me unless old Doyle sent them in. The manager, he'd come around some, but Mr. Doyle, he told the manager to kind of leave me alone to be learning for myself. I got paid two hundred fifty dollars a month, and the use of some old furniture, but I sure did learn a lot. I was up on my horse at three some mornings, trying to do a good job for old Mr. Doyle, who'd put so much trust in me. It wasn't like today, when they call nearly

101

anybody that wears a hat a cowboy—and pay them for it, too. But I was doing what I wanted, and I don't believe a person's got to be paid all the time for everything he does if he's learning from it. It's like I'd tell Betsy—if we was paid more, we never would've learned so much.

"Course, Betsy thought old Mr. Doyle was right mean. He'd drive up in his Cadillac, and if he didn't like something he'd cuss me out and stamp his foot and throw a right mean tantrum. Betsy said he had no respect. But he had psychology, that's what he had. And he knew cattle better than anyone I ever knew. I didn't make him near a good enough hand. It took me years to see how I never would have known nothing like I do now without him using that psychology—leaving me alone for two, three months and then driving up in that expensive car and cussing me out. Course, it was hard on Betsy. She was lonesome, I guess, with no women around to talk to. And it must of made her nervous, being way out there with a baby to look after and the twins on the way and no water for diapers, no electricity or telephone or nothing. Why, we was so far from anything that when those old twins was near born, the doctor, he told me to carry around a clean white shoestring, in case I had to cut the cord. Betsy got so nervous then she got her mother to come on out and pull—I mean, help her have Pearl and Laurie. Course, Betsy had her home and her babies, and that's everything a woman should need. And I tried to be real good to her. There was only one time I hit her. I swatted her with a rope—I never did hit a woman openhanded. But, like I said, she was alone most all the time, except for the babies.

"I'd talk to Betsy about the kids and the house and all

them things you talk to a wife about. But riding around all day alone—that suited me fine and it still suits me fine. I don't know what lonesome means, and I'd rather be a-horseback, thinking, than talking to a woman. Cowboys don't like the company of women much. We don't really have much in common with them. A cowboy figures that when a man gets old he's got plenty of time then to sit around in some old rocking chair talking to his wife. Course, there's Calvin Pratt—he talks over all his business with Annabel, but he's really a farmer. I know one thing sure—if a man is a sure-enough cowpuncher, he don't want no woman knowing his business. Like I tell Betsy—'This ranch, it's none of your business. It's *my* job, *my* worry.' Seems to me if you start talking to a woman she thinks she knows what's going on. It's something that just comes natural to a woman. Course, some is different. Like Em Smith. What I admire about old Em is she don't ever say nothing in front of people to make them think she's the boss. And Betsy's like that. She never complained much, out there on Mr. Doyle's ranch. She was willing to work hard so as I could accomplish something, and she never took no credit. If I needed neighboring real bad, and Mr. Doyle sent some of his hands in—why, I could leave instructions with Betsy and she'd always give them right. She'd say, 'Henry wants you to do this.' Or 'Henry wants you to do that.' Where lots of women would say, '*I* want this done.'

"Like Betsy says, those were the happiest days she had, out there on that old ranch. We was working for the future, because old Mr. Doyle, he had offered me this deal. It was toward spring, in '60 or '61. Old Doyle, he drove up one day and we visited some, and Betsy cooked this real nice lunch. And afterward old Doyle says that maybe it's time I got started on my own. The deal was this—that next fall he'd let me cut out fifty head of heifer calves from the herd and pay for them when they had calves. What I mean is, for every steer those heifers had at their first calving, I'd trade old Doyle the steer for ownership of the heifer. And it wouldn't cost me nothing to run them, he said. I could use those cows—they was registered Hereford, and you got near five hundred dollars apiece for a registered Hereford back then. I could use those cows as collateral on some homestead land and get my own spread going. Oh, we was real excited about that. Betsy wrote to her folks and then to mine and said we was going to be ranchers. And her mother wrote back offering a little money she'd been saving up to help us out. But then old Doyle, he up and died that summer. And his children sold every bit of his land.

"Course, they didn't know about our deal. I mean, it was just a deal between him and me—I don't know as his wife even knew about it. Mr. Doyle, he had offered me a contract back when we first talked about it, but I said, 'Shoot, if a man's got to make a contract!' I said, 'Mr. Doyle, the way I was raised, a man's word is good as any contract,' and I could see he was real pleased, 'cause that's the way he was raised, too. So when he died, course I got nothing. Old Mrs. Doyle, she came calling once or twice, but we wouldn't say nothing to her. It's like with Lester and my percentage of the gross here. I know what's due me, and Betsy says I should be asking about that money—like asking to see the ranch books. But, hell, a man don't ask that. And it was the same with Mrs. Doyle. We had a deal, Doyle and me, and it was something just between us, and it didn't work out, and it wasn't nobody else's problem.

"Seems like we moved around a lot after that. Five ranches in seven years before I got this here job. It's just that no place seemed right—I mean, it always seemed like we was having to start out all over. I'd be working on a ranch. Some was good, but most—well, the yearling men were getting in and they treated their hands like something sub-human. So I'd be there working hard with someone else's cattle, and I'd get to thinking that if old Mr. Doyle was alive those heifers of mine would be dropping their first calves, or those heifers would be old mama cows by now and I'd have bought some land and . . . It sure is strange. Some guys I know—one of them got himself a deal running six thousand head for one of them rich Arabs. And there's another that just walked into the bank one day when the manager must of felt real good, 'cause he walked out with enough money for ten sections down in Mexico. Now, I know it's not so important for a man to be top deal, but sometimes I get to thinking that I could of raised up four girls and worn out a couple of saddles and got to be forty years old in the time it took to get another chance to have some cattle of my own."

Chapter 10

HENRY tried to cover the Willow Ranch every week in his pickup, and he almost always found work for himself somewhere. Summers, when the sun had cured the grass to a dry, tough scrub, the problem was usually water. There were sixty-seven windmills on the Willow Ranch, and it was up to Henry to keep those sixty-seven windmills pumping. Winters, the problem was cows, grazing a crooked way across the ranch's biggest pastures. Henry had to find them and mark their whereabouts on a ranch map, so that his hands, heading out in the morning with the daily feed cake, knew where to go. In early spring, calves were born, and there were always fence posts torn up by the spring rains which needed sinking. And now, in May, with yearlings coming off winter wheat, it was time to

106

start checking pastures—time to test the grass for summer grazing and make a decision as to where the different cattle on the ranch belonged. Henry could remember checking pastures with his grandfathers back in the days before cowboys drove around in pickups. A foreman rode so much in those days that he usually took a string of ten or fifteen fresh horses to make the rounds of a ranch the size of the Willow. Henry himself got by with only three or four horses. He rode, of course, when he was roping and dragging calves at brandings, or when he was sorting cattle or moving a herd from one pasture to another. There were places, too, where a pickup was useless. No pickup could get down into a caliche gully and flush a wayward cow, or drive a lost calf out of the corner of a pasture where cactus and bear grass and mesquite had conspired to make the brush tortuous. And a lot of the work that felt proper to a man on horseback simply seemed comical and laborious when it was done behind the wheel of a truck.

Still, Henry was used to a truck by now. He figured that over the last nine years he had put in more time breaking in his string of pickup trucks than he had ever spent breaking in his horses, and each of those trucks had been as personal to him as a favored horse. He had shaped them to his needs and his temperament, the way he had trained Pepper as a colt, until they suited him precisely. People could look at Henry's newest pickup and know in a minute that it belonged to him. They could do the same with any cowboy's pickup: with Tom Blanton's, which was a friendly, muddled sort of truck, with its stash of cookies and candy bars and sugar cubes and his children's abandoned toys; or with Calvin Pratt's pickup, which was such an orderly, cau-

107

tious truck, with its box of requisitions and receipts, its snakebite kit, its labelled satchels full of fence-mending tools, and the neat row of hooks along the sides where Calvin hung his booster cable, his air pump, his pruning saw, and his shovels. Henry's truck at the moment was a 1976 Ford—three-quarter ton, painted red, and already scraped and a little shabby. The cab floor was littered with old receipts and crumpled notes from Henry's scratch pad, and at least half a dozen mismatched pairs of fence-mending gloves were piled on the dashboard, next to his pint of bourbon. In the back of the truck, there was always a paper bag full of canned sardines, sausages, and chili, along with a big metal water jug, Henry's Winchester rifle, a thermos to keep his bourbon cool in the summer, and a horse blanket and quilted parka to use at night, winters, if the truck broke down. Some of his tools had been dumped in an old feed bucket which already held an assortment of odds and ends that changed trucks whenever he did—old bridle bits, a roll of rattlesnake-fence wire, a hammerhead without a handle, a single boot. The rest of his tools were handy, as he put it—which meant they were lying all over the truck floor, getting rusty. They gave the truck a bleak, neglected look, but that look had seemed to suit Henry's spirits over the past few years. Now that he had made his deal with Lester Hill and was on his way to a fortune, he kept meaning to straighten up his truck—to sort the tools, get rid of the debris. It was just something he never got around to. He still drove off on his rounds with everything aboard except the tools he needed most. He was apt to forget his shovel or the giant pair of pliers he used for tightening fences, and have to drive back to the barn to get them,

108

muttering and killing time. This morning—five miles out on his rounds, towing Pepper in the horse trailer—he stopped to check a windmill well and discovered that he had left his pump jack at home. He was heading in when Lester signalled on the two-way radio.

"You there?" Lester's voice crackled.

Henry mashed the button, scowling.

"Don't know who else it'd be," Henry said softly.

"What?"

Henry shrugged. "Yeah, it's me."

"Just checking in," Lester said. There was a low chuckle. "Don't call for a bit—hear? I'm going back up. Get myself a little you-know-what."

Henry switched off, wincing. That was the way his manager liked to talk to cowboys, and there was not much that Henry could do about it except wince and assume that talking coarse to a cowboy must make Lester feel like one himself. Most of the hands just figured that Lester was a little perverted. There was a rumor in town that Lester liked to come home at night, all sweaty and filthy from working cattle or prowling around some feedyard, and drag his dainty Pennsylvania wife upstairs to bed. Henry had disputed the rumor for a while, since he knew for a fact that Lester never left his Buick if there was a cow within a hundred yards, but then word got around that Henry was Lester's boy, and when that happened Henry stopped arguing. What really bothered him about Lester anyway was that Lester sat in his Buick drinking expensive bourbon and never offering his men a drop. Henry used to let Lester know how he felt about the bourbon; he did it by completely ignoring Lester whenever Lester was around.

109

Lester longed for attention from his cowboys. He wanted Henry to admire him, but Henry figured that Lester needed him too much to start complaining about hurt feelings, and, as it happened, Henry was right. Lester was a Texas boy, but he had no notion of what should be ordered for a ranch or what the right price was or even who was a reliable supplier. He did not know much about evaluating cattle, either, even after four years at Cornell University's agricultural school. There had been times when Henry was ready to tell Lester off—but that was before they made their deal. Now they were partners, to Henry's way of thinking, and Henry felt a kind of responsibility to be polite.

"It's a hard thing for me, being that fellow in the middle," Henry said after he had found his jack and was heading out again on a bumpy cowpath to the ranch's north pastures. "It's like you're responsible but at the same time you got no authority. Take them cows." He pointed out the window to a herd of cows watering at the big round stock tanks near a wooden windmill. "I know in my own mind that a lot of things ought to be done different with them cows. I know there's some over there that needs selling. Last year, I had them bad ones all cut out for shipping, but Lester, he never did ship them, and now them cows is right back eating up the grass. To my mind, if that old cow over there don't produce, she shouldn't be eating up that grass another season. They wouldn't keep me around for long, or one of the horses, if we didn't produce. That's what I keep telling Lester—we should always be calving more heifers than we need, and always be culling. The ones that done that, they've been real successful ranchers. But Lester never does like to listen."

Henry had turned off the path to scatter salt licks. The cows, which had backed off at the sound of his horn, came padding toward the truck now, expecting feed cake. Henry got out, looked them over, and made a mental note of the ones without a calf suckling. Then he walked over to the windmill with his pump jack. He had seen from the truck that the water in the tanks was low, and now, jacking up the rod that drew that water up from three hundred and fifty feet below the ground and stretching out on his belly in the mud, he put his ear to the raised rod and listened. He said he always had trouble with the windmills in this pasture. The wells beneath them were drying up, and none of those wells could be deepened, because the casing on their pipes was too small to accommodate drilling tools. Larger casings would have solved the problem, but they were expensive, and Lester refused to buy them, even when a well dried up entirely and he had to have a new one dug. The most that Henry could do under the circumstances was to keep the checks working and the windmills repaired, and pray that the water lasted out the season. It saddened Henry, because he loved windmills. He loved to see their blades whirring in a good breeze, and fresh, cold water pouring into their stock tanks. He was proud of his skill with windmills. It was a skill he had taught himself, over years of listening to slender pipes for the subtle and intricate sounds of trouble hundreds of feet beneath him. He had never been farther from home than Arizona, but today, at the windmill, he announced that once he'd made his money he was going to visit Holland, which had the best windmills in the world.

"This sure is one pretty pasture, with all them windmills," he went on, starting the truck. "Lester had some of them government specialists in a few years back and they said this pasture was way too big. They said you got to have small pastures, so you can look after the cattle better, feed them better. But I argued that if you give a mama cow plenty of room she'll go her natural right way. If a pasture's big enough—why, it might rain on one part and not on the other, and those old cows, they'll just move with the weather and the good grazing in their own time, and you won't have to go gathering them in whenever there's a little problem. You can let them alone and gather twice a year —which sure is enough gathering, if you ask them cows."

Henry drove on, talking, to the next pasture. The grass was greener there. It was growing close and thick, and Henry stopped the pickup and jumped down for a better look. "There's just no way to see from a truck the way you see afoot or a-horseback," he said, breaking a couple of blades and sniffing them. "I'm kind of watching this grass. It's had a rest since last October—everything here kind of gets a rest, certain times. And now it's growing real good, and I'm going to put some cattle on it." Henry stood up, grinning. He said he was thinking about the calves that he and Lester were going to sell—his birthday calves, Betsy and Melinda called them. The calves were in one of the small south pastures now, in sight of headquarters, but Henry figured they would do much better on this stout, nutritious grass.

"It used to be you sold cattle by the head, big or little," Henry said. "Course, now it's all computers and futures that determines prices, but the care of them's still the same. There's no rancher yet can get along without a good cowboy, unless he's one himself. A lot of them ranchers think that if a cowboy's running cattle of his own they'll lose him. You'd of thought they'd know how much money it takes to go into the cattle business. Course, things is getting better now. They got retirement plans and real good health insurance at most ranches, and there's a lot of them starting those percentage deals. But, still, there's a part of a rancher's attitude that says taking care of a cowboy is just like taking care of a good slave before the Civil War. If you make some rancher a good hand, he'll likely see you don't go hungry when you're old, but mostly an old cowboy's like an old horse to him—no matter how much he's liked you, even if you've made him the best hand in the world, he's going to put you out to pasture soon as you get to be a burden to him."

Henry stopped the truck suddenly. "See that cow?" he said, pointing. "She's looking for her calf. It's kind of hard to explain, exactly, but a cow with a calf on her—there's something about her. You can just tell." Henry waited. In a few minutes, a tiny calf came skittering out from behind a cactus. The cow stared hard at the pickup. She lowed for her baby and kept on lowing until it had skittered past the truck and was nestled underneath her, suckling, but she never once took her eyes off the pickup until her baby was safe. Henry chuckled and drove off, talking about cows. He said that the hardest thing about moving mama cows was making certain every mama had her calf. Calvin Pratt was good at that. He had patience and let a cow take her time finding her baby. But Ed Loomis, with his wildness— Henry shook his head. He never let Ed near his mama cows, because Ed was so fond of galloping around and roping every animal he saw. There were gentler ways of moving cows, Henry said. Sometimes he took one of the milk cows from the barn and tied a cowbell to her neck; then the herd would follow calmly. Sometimes he got down on the ground himself and lowed and lowed until the cows gathered—but that was something he felt a little foolish doing.

It was nearly noon when Henry stopped again. The sun was high now, and the air came in hot blasts through the open windows of the cab and hung there, dusty and stifling. Henry had been driving with his gloves on since ten o'clock, when the steering wheel began to burn his hands. He had eaten lunch, driving—a couple of packs of peanut-butter crackers and a Hershey bar—but he had forgotten to fill his jug back at the windmill, and he had just cut across a weaning pasture to the bunkhouse for a glass of water. His three Mexican hands, who were already taking their siestas, woke up when they heard his horn. They stood at the bunkhouse door, blinking and yawning, and in a minute another Mexican, who was a stranger to Henry, joined them.

This new Mexican—each of the bunkhouse hands, in turn, swore he was his cousin—had crossed the border alone a week ago. He had made his way to the Panhandle, travelling nights, and now, evidently, he was hiding out in the bunkhouse while Henry's hands asked around about work for him on a friendly ranch. Wetback wages were five dollars a day, at most, in the Panhandle, and for those wages Mexican hands were expected to do the jobs that none of the Texas cowboys liked doing. They cleaned the barns. They sank fence posts. Sometimes they hauled and scattered feed cake. But they were not allowed on horseback at most ranches—the opinion in west Texas being that Mexicans were cruel to animals. There were ranches in south Texas—along the Rio Grande or in the Gulf Coast archipelago—where all the cowboys were Mexican. In south Texas, wetback hands, working for chattels' pay and under conditions of appalling squalor, rode and roped and tended cattle, but in the Panhandle a man on horseback was supposed to be a "white" man, even if a white man cost more.

There was a time, just after Reconstruction, when a lot of the Panhandle's range hands were black. They were freed slaves, mainly, who had come west in the seventies and eighties, and for a while some of their sons and grandsons stayed on to cowboy, too. Henry's Granddaddy Wesley once rode with a black cowboy. He liked to talk about the summer they had worked a line camp together—they were both boys then, and they would sit up half the night swapping ghost stories, but when the time came for sleeping, the black boy would always excuse himself politely and lay his bedroll on the ground outdoors while Wesley settled down to the relative comfort of a cot in the line-camp shed. Henry had met that black cowboy once, when he himself was nine or ten and the cowboy was well past seventy. There was a dinner in Amarillo honoring the old Panhandle cowpunchers, and Henry had gone to the dinner with his Granddaddy Wesley and his Granddaddy Abel and sat proudly with the men at a big banquet table shaped like a horseshoe. He never forgot the way the old black hand had stood at the back of the room all through the dinner and the speeches, smiling gratefully whenever his name figured in a story. That night, Granddaddy Wesley had proposed

115

a toast to him—"If there's a nigger Heaven, old Amos here will be the first one in," Wesley said—and even now, years after Amos died in a shack in northwest Amarillo, people still talked with great feeling about how proper and respectful Amos was. Amos, in fact, was one of the last black cowboys in the Panhandle. Those who could get out did. Those who stayed had long since fled the range for the slums of Amarillo, where, according to Henry, they drank all day and plotted crimes of considerable fiendishness against defenseless cowboy families. But the truth was that no black man with any sense showed up on a Panhandle ranch without a good reason for being there, and cowboys north of the Canadian River, where sentiment ran high and primitive, liked to boast that no black man could spend a night in *their* part of the country and count on leaving alive in the morning.

It was hardly surprising that by Henry's time there were few blacks left in the Panhandle with any appetite for cowboying. Mexicans had replaced them as the woebegone factotums on the big ranches, and ranch talk nowadays ran to keeping Mexicans respectful. Henry's Mexican hands were named Juan, Pedro, and Fortunato—Henry had trouble with their last names—and Henry often said that they were a good example of Mexicans who knew their place. Actually, their patience and inscrutable good humor made him feel awkward. They were so agreeable that Henry was fairly certain they were making fun of him. Something about the way they looked bothered him. They were meticulously dapper. They wore their Mexican cowboy clothes and their gleaming *mostachos* like jewelry. Their tight fawn trousers, their patent-leather boots and fake

116

Stetsons seemed to Henry a kind of mockery of his own. He rarely went into the bunkhouse. Today, he stayed in the pickup while Fortunato got the water and Pedro, talking half in English and half in Spanish, went through a cheerful monologue of family tragedies—of hungry children and sick mothers and aging spinster sisters in need of dowries.

Henry drove off, muttering to himself. He had promised the new cousin a month's board at the bunkhouse in exchange for some work sinking fence posts, and now he regretted it, though not enough to turn around. He was eager to see his birthday calves, near headquarters, and he drove as fast as he could now, raising clouds of dust and lurching across the path until Pepper, whinnying in the trailer, slowed him down. The path led to the Willow's western boundary, then turned and followed the boundary south for a few miles before it dipped toward headquarters. Henry stopped once to make a note about calling the foreman at the Triple R, next door, and setting a date to inspect their joint fence. Texas fence laws were peculiar. The law was clear for farmers—farmers in Texas who wanted to protect their fields from a neighboring rancher's cattle had to fence those cattle out, and it did them no good to complain to Austin that there were a lot of states in the country where ranchers were obliged to fence their cattle *in*. But a fence between ranchers was considered something of a sacred trust. Texas would not offend its cattlemen by interfering in the sort of business that cattlemen, as men of honor, had always settled among themselves with a firm handshake and a toast, and consequently it was impossible to tell from any of the fencing statutes who was responsible for a broken fence between ranches—or even, sometimes, who owned that fence in the first place.

When Henry first came to the Willow, he and the fore-man at the Triple R had spent a few years waiting for each other to repair the fence they shared, and the result had been that each of them put in a lot of time rounding up the other's cattle. Now they had an arrangement. Every year, they settled on a day in June when they both rode out with their hands to inspect the year's damage, and over the next week or so they shared the work and the cost of the repairs. Lately, though, the owner of the Triple R had taken up raising bulls in the pasture that adjoined the Willow. They were enormous bulls—big, expensive Brangus, from a breeder herd near Borger—and Henry, who was running a lot of heifers this year, worried about his neighbor's bulls' jumping the fence and working the heifers till their backs broke. The fence already sagged in places, and the earth around it was trampled where some of the bulls had tried to jump. Henry said that to his mind there was nothing quite so fearsome as the sight of a randy bull confronting a cow across a four-tier barbed-wire fence—unless, of course, it was the sight of an angry cowboy in a pickup, with one hand banging on the horn and the other banging on the door, trying to drive that bull away. Henry had stopped again, about a mile down the south boundary, to tighten a sagging wire. Suddenly he threw his pliers down and pointed to a line of bulls in the distance, approaching the fence with the slow and ominous precision of a column of black tanks. He was frowning, and then he shrugged, and then he smiled. They were handsome bulls, he said. Maybe he would raise some bulls like those himself once his ranch got started. One of these days, he would have a grandson.

With his own bulls, he could teach the boy a thing or two about roping.

Henry talked all the way home. By the time he reached the little pasture where his birthday calves were grazing, he was full of schemes for the future. The calves looked good —healthy and gaining—and it was hard to imagine them as the scabby, scouring Okies that Sam Otis had prodded down the chute less than a month ago. Henry led Pepper out of the trailer. For a while, he rode the pasture, sitting tall and praising everything his calves did. That evening, after supper, he told Betsy that it might be nice to take their iced tea out behind the barn and watch the sunset.

Chapter 11

LATELY, Betsy Blanton had been thinking a lot about loneliness. She felt it coming on, like gray hair or another wedding anniversary or a new tornado season. She began to dwell on memories of when the girls were small and she was always too busy cooking and ironing and worrying over colds and broken bones to fret about herself. In memory, the isolation of her life then never bothered her. Daughters, after all, were the best company a wife could have. Her mother had told her that just before her wedding, and she had prayed for a daughter during each of her three pregnancies—though she never mentioned those prayers to Henry, and was even a little ashamed of them herself, because she suspected that praying for things like daughters or oil wells was something

Catholics did. Her cousin Madge had married a Catholic, to the family's horror, and he had in fact struck oil. His well came in on a useless section over the Oklahoma border that he was trying to farm for alfalfa, and now Madge had ten million dollars, a swimming pool, a little blue airplane of her own, and a stack of gold and diamond bracelets for each arm. Betsy liked Madge. Twice a year, they met in Amarillo and had a fancy lunch at the city's second-best country club —not the Amarillo Country Club, where the old ranching families went, but the Tascosa Country Club, where rich cattle traders and people who had just got their oil showed off. Betsy always had a fine time with Madge, and forgot how nervous she had been about her clothes and her hair and what to order. She was not a jealous woman. She liked to say that Madge got the oil and she got the daughters, and that just showed how the good Lord always divided up His blessings fair and proper.

Three of Betsy's girls were gone now. Mattie had married a cowboy and moved to a ranch in Colorado. And Betsy's twins, Laurie and Pearl, who were so good at basketball and track, along with having been the first girls in the history of the district high school to make the grass-judging team —they had left for the University of Texas last fall on scholarships. Melinda, of course, was still at home. She had three more years of high school, and, as Betsy always said, she was a good Christian girl. Actually, Melinda had inherited some of the extraordinary ardor that ran through the Blanton family, and just this spring, to her mother's bewilderment, had been so taken with the Holy Spirit at a revival meeting at the rodeo grounds near town that she had started to shake ecstatically and talk in tongues. Betsy could

121

not really complain about her youngest daughter. Melinda got her homework in on time, and ran for the girls' track team, and twirled a baton to her mother's credit. Her report cards were always good, and to Betsy's knowledge she had never been sent to the principal's office, where blasphemers, smokers, and kissers now had a choice of three strokes of the principal's yardstick or a month of hard work after school.

But Melinda was not much company to her mother anymore. She was silent and mysterious lately. She came home from school, fed the horses and put the dogies on the milk cows, and then disappeared into her bedroom. She seemed to divide her time between homework, romance magazines, and the Bible. She was as fervent about boys now as she was about Jesus, and in a way she combined her passions with an enviable efficiency. She had a cache of makeup and fingernail polish in the dresser drawer where she kept her slide rule, her science notebooks, and her collection of transcripts of revival-meeting testimonies. Her biggest problem at the moment was whether, as a Christian, she would put her immortal soul in jeopardy by going to the Friday-night socials at the Catholic parish hall. It was a real problem, the Catholics being the only people around who held regular teen-age dances, but by now it was more theological than practical, since Henry refused to discuss it and had whipped her soundly with his belt the one time she tried to argue with him about going.

Betsy wished that Melinda and Henry got along better, the way they had when Melinda was a little girl. It used to please her, seeing them together. They looked so much alike—Melinda was big, like her father, with the same gray eyes and sandy hair. But Henry seemed uncomfortable, and even embarrassed, around Melinda now that she was fourteen. It was something that happened to cowboys when their daughters started growing up. Cowboys preferred their daughters small. They doted on them then. They loved making cowhands of their frisky little girls—they took them riding and roping and rodeoing, and showed them off to all their friends. Henry used to say that Melinda was his best hand. He gave her a big black hat like his, and on Saturday mornings the two of them would put their hats on and disappear—and Betsy would worry till they rode home at dinnertime, battered and scratched and full of gruesome stories. But Henry had not had one of his Saturdays with Melinda in the last two years. It did not seem right to him any longer. He had given Melinda a merry childhood out-of-doors, and then Melinda was returned to her mother as abruptly and unexpectedly as she had been put on a pony for her first ride at the age of three. Betsy had looked forward to that day, what with her other girls growing up. Mattie and the twins, at Melinda's age, had been her confidantes—more her sisters, she always said, than her daughters—and the kitchen then was thick with giggles and conspiracies and secret talk. Of course, Betsy had had more time for her girls before she started working. Now, with a job so far from home, she got back at night with barely enough time to cook the supper. The kitchen seemed too quiet to her lately. And when she knocked at her daughter's door at ten to say goodnight, and saw the pink bedroom, with its soft lights and organdie ruffles, that she had copied so faithfully from her fantasies of a perfect girlhood, she could not help thinking that the room would be empty soon.

A few years back, Betsy began to cry in bed at night. She would wait for Henry to hear her. She wanted him to wake up when she cried, to comfort her when she said that she was lonely. But Henry, not knowing much about comforting, usually laughed nervously and tried to say something cheerful—something like "This country's good for a man and a cow, honey, but it's always been hell on a mule or a woman"—and then Betsy would cry some more. Soon she was crying all the time. She was alone most days, having done her job so well that the sorghum dealer let his other clerk go. Saturdays, she had to clean the house and do the laundry. And that left only Saturday nights—when Henry was willing—and Sundays for dry eyes and real company. Then, last fall, Betsy's appendix burst. She spent two weeks in the hospital, and by the end of those two weeks she was having such a wonderful time visiting up and down the corridors, talking to people about their troubles, that when the doctor dismissed her she begged him to let her stay. She told the doctor she was grieving. He looked puzzled for a moment, but then he smiled and said that she should take up "serious reading," because it was clear, as he put it, that Betsy was an intelligent woman, only more sensitive than some. Later that day, at the town library, Betsy asked for serious books about women grieving. She tried a novel called "The Bell Jar," which was shocking to her and difficult to understand, and when she returned it, asking for another, the librarian said that as far as she knew "The Bell Jar" was the only serious book about grieving women the

124

library had. The librarian recommended Victor Hugo, Charles Dickens, and James Michener, whose books were too long. Then she recommended poets, Keats, Shelley, Browning—Betsy checked them out, read them, and returned them. Then she discovered Kahlil Gibran. She loved Gibran. She bought her own copy of "The Prophet," and even started reading it out loud to Henry at night after supper. She hoped that the words would move him and make him tender. They made him bored and fidgety instead.

Betsy kept on reading her Gibran. He gave her strength, she said. But in the end he didn't help her with a brooding husband who either sat up half the night watching television Westerns or drove off to town and caroused and drank. She went to her preacher for advice next. She said to him, "Reverend, I'm tired of grieving when no one's died." The preacher thought about that, looking puzzled the way the doctor had. Finally, he told Betsy that her life would definitely change for the better if she persuaded her husband to come to church with her. There was a lot of arguing about churchgoing at the Blantons' that night. Betsy said she *liked* the idea of having a husband next to her in church Sundays. Henry, as usual, said that *his* church was the great outdoors. Then Betsy said that if Henry thought the great outdoors was a church, he was misinformed—and the result was that Henry stormed out of the house and started toasting nature from the driver's seat of his grandfather's chuck wagon. Betsy, in tears, called the Smiths. George had just dozed off with the latest *Calf News*, but Emily told Betsy to drop everything, get in the car, and meet her at the ranch gate, and then she left a note for

George: "Chaperoning Betsy. Go to bed."

The women drove around for an hour and a half, and ended up in the dance lounge of a Pampa motel. It was Emily's idea to make Henry jealous with a night out, and it had sounded like a good idea to Betsy until she got to the lounge and discovered herself in a dark room full of noisy salesmen and of women in low-cut blouses who sat alone at little tables waiting for company. Betsy was terrified. She forced herself to drink a Daiquiri—Daiquiris were Emily Smith's favorite cocktail—and even to dance with a young salesman from Lubbock who had a wedding ring on his finger, but when the man put his lips to her ear and whispered, "Room Eleven," she ran out of the lounge and waited in the car for Emily to pay the bill. The worst part of her adventure, she said later, was coming home at two-thirty in the morning ready for a thrilling scene and finding Henry in bed, peacefully snoring. Henry was so full of sweet bourbon dreams that night that when Betsy joined him he smiled graciously in his sleep and moved over to give her room.

Annabel Pratt scolded Betsy about her adventure when they were having coffee in the church rectory after Bible class that Sunday. Annabel and Calvin played canasta with the Smiths once a month, but Annabel did not really approve of Emily Smith and her influence. A perfect home— tidy and soothing, like the home she had made for Calvin during *his* troubles—was what Annabel recommended. And so for the next few months Betsy was busy painting and polishing, sewing and shopping. She went to the bank and withdrew the money she had been saving for her Christmas clothes. She cancelled her weekly appointment at the Pampa beauty parlor. She started skipping lunch. Saturdays, now, she drove for hours to compare the prices of chintz and paints and wallpaper at the big country discount centers. Sundays, she stayed at home, scraping furniture and piecing together carpet remnants for a new rug.

Betsy's house on the Willow Ranch was small and not very solidly constructed. It had no basement, and Betsy, who worried about tornadoes, had kept it spare and simple, as if she half expected it to blow away one day. She had the example of the Smiths' houses, and the house that Henry's parents lost to a twister twenty years ago. No house was safe, really, whether it was in town or in the country. A tornado that hit Lefors in the spring of 1975 destroyed sixty of the town's houses. Five years earlier, a twister cut an eight-mile path through Lubbock. It came down on the city with such speed and such force that the warning siren was never sounded. Lubbock was devastated and twenty-six people were killed. There were rules to follow in tornado season. Pressure could explode a sealed house during a tornado, and so whenever a warning was out for the Willow the first thing Betsy did was open all the doors and windows. Then she let the horses and the milk cows out of the barn, packed her picture album and a few of her favorite things in a suitcase, called whoever was at home, and tried to outdrive the storm. She knew that the men, out in the pastures, would find a creek or a gully to protect them, but to her mind a flimsy prefabricated ranch house was no place to wait out a tornado—even though Annabel Pratt maintained that a person was always safe in the bathtub or under a bed, covered with mattresses. Some cowboys' wives crawled under their houses, but rattlesnakes nested under the Blantons' house, and Betsy had never tried it. There was a time when Betsy could kill a rattler with a shovel or a stick and think nothing of it. Now that she was older, she was too frightened of snakes to get that close to one, and so she used Henry's shotgun, reasoning that age and motherhood made every woman cautious. She was scared of coyotes, too. Years ago, she had found a coyote, sluggish with rabies, camped on her doorstep a few yards from where the twins were playing with their dolls.

Once Betsy started decorating, she changed her mind about tornadoes. As she explained it to Henry, they had survived nine years on the Willow and watched a hundred tornadoes gathering above the pastures, and the house was still standing. Now there was a lot for her to do, she told him, because the girls' room was the only room she had ever really fixed up. She began with the bathroom. Two satiny blue shower curtains went up, drawn back on either side with velvet bows to frame the bathtub. Soon plastic ivy drooped from the ceiling. Plastic chrysanthemums, in little gilt pots, sat precariously around the rim of the washbasin and the tub. The room took on a wet, heady smell, which came from steaming bathwater and too much Airwick Herbal Bouquet, and one morning, after searching in the mist for half an hour, Henry was horrified to discover his toothbrush in a bud vase and his razor and shaving soap in a Maxwell House coffee can disguised by grosgrain ribbon and paper lace. He complained for a while. He did not like having to take his boots off at the bathroom door, either, but Betsy insisted that boots, and even shoes, would damage the new shag rug.

Betsy was full of enthusiasm by then. She stripped the

varnish off her old bedroom set and painted it antique white with gold trim. She made bedroom curtains out of a bolt of filmy white nylon with golden pineapples on the border that she had found for a dollar a yard on one of her shopping Saturdays. She bought a big scented candle to replace the white china bull—it was a Charolais—that Henry's brother Tom had wired as a bedside lamp on the Blantons' fifteenth wedding anniversary. Then she took on the parlor. In one weekend, she waxed the upright piano that Henry had bought for eighty dollars at a Pampa bar closing, selected two bucolic landscapes from one of her mail-order catalogues, painted the bookcase that held Henry's rodeo trophies, and took the rest of the furniture out behind the barn and stained it fruitwood brown. The next weekend, she was at the sewing machine again. She made ruffled curtains out of a pretty green-and-yellow wild-flower chintz, and then she made matching slipcovers for the couch and the rocker, a ruffled cushion for the piano seat, and a ruffled cloth for the little round table where she kept her *Woman's Days* and *Reader's Digests* and Henry his *Western Horsemans* and *TV Guides*. By Christmas, the house was ready. Betsy had stayed up late every night for a week finishing the kitchen. It was a proper ranch kitchen—it took up half the house, with the three other rooms opening off it like afterthoughts—and had a big round table by the window, where twelve hands could sit down comfortably to a branding lunch. Betsy had oiled the table till the oak shone, painted the walls yellow, and scrubbed everything in sight, from her storage freezer to Henry's windowsill collection of ceramic cows.

Finally, Betsy had driven down to the best supermarket.

129

in Pampa and stocked the kitchen with the family's favorite food. Ranch people like Betsy were proud of the food they bought in supermarkets—food that came in cans and packages and bottles that squirted their contents out of complicated spouts. Betsy kept her own mesquite-bean preserves in the kitchen cupboard, but she saw to it that her jams and cereals and steak sauces from the supermarket were always on display on a big revolving tray in the middle of the kitchen table. She marketed with a kind of reverence. Choosing food from the abundant shelves of a supermarket, wheeling her cart to the graceful beat of the piped music, watching her bright pile of cans and boxes grow— those were things that made Betsy feel connected to the world and almost prosperous. The cream from the milk cows in the barn was fine for everyday. So were the wild strawberries from the patch behind the house. But for a holiday like Christmas Betsy wanted to be able to offer frozen strawberries and to set out cans of Reddi Wip and coffee creamer on her revolving tray. Her spread on Christmas Eve was elegant. There was a big pot roast simmering in its juices in the oven. New bottles of steak sauce and salad dressing and Dr Pepper glittered on the table, and the Christmas candles cast warm shadows on the yellow walls. Pearl and Laurie had just arrived that afternoon from college. They helped Betsy take the tangled strings of Christmas lights down from the top of the broom closet, and then Melinda laid them carefully beside the thick blue spruce that was sitting in a tub at the kitchen window, waiting to be trimmed. At six, they all sat down at the table and listened for the sound of Henry's pickup. By seven, Betsy was getting angry. By eight, she was worried and the pot roast was ruined. She was crying when the phone finally rang at nine-thirty, and Tom's wife, Lisa Lou, in a voice stiff with bitterness, announced that she had had a call from a bar in town.

"It's not that I didn't sympathize," Betsy said on the day Henry moved his birthday calves to his favorite pasture. Betsy was so excited that day that she had called in sick and stayed home from work to cook a special lunch for all the cowhands. "Henry and Tom, they said they had important business over in town, and, like Lisa Lou said, from the racket on the telephone she just knew that business was drinking. But now I figure that Henry maybe couldn't *face* Christmas. Here he was, fixing to be forty years old. I mean, he always thought he'd have a place in life. He set a goal and a time, and it was getting near that time, and it looked to him like he wasn't going to make it. So he wasn't happy. It's funny. All I ever wanted was him—just him and the girls and some good times. That's what would've made me happy, and I never did know why men aren't content with the same things. Maybe some men are, but not cowboys. Course, I'm right proud of Henry for cowboying. I'm proud of all the men that do. I look at them and I feel a sort of smugness, and, you know, a ranch is the best place in the world for kids. Even those places we lived with no conveniences—it was always a good, clean life for the girls.

"And as for Henry's being a cowboy, I'm sure he always planned it. Back when he was five or six and couldn't even get off his horse—he had to back up to a fence or that old chair he talks about. Even then, he liked being alone a-horseback. I remember when Henry took that first cowboying job with Mr. Doyle. He was so excited—even with all

131

our troubles, like leaving school, and a new baby, and having to sell our car. So I was real excited, too. I thought it was going to be a nice adventure, and I enjoyed it, because Henry was starting out and doing what he wanted to. Course, I was the dumbest thing you ever saw then. When I started dating Henry, I guess I thought if we was married Henry would take care of me. Henry was a hero. I kind of think he expected to be a hero all his life. At the beginning, he'd come home from a rodeo all black and blue, but he'd be proud of himself, 'cause he'd be carrying this big trophy. Once, I remember, the boys had a wild-mare race, and one of those old mares just about kicked Henry to death. But Henry came home grinning. It was 'cause he'd *won*. Being a hero—that's what made him generous and loving. We were making only two-fifty or three hundred a month then, and Mattie and Pearl and Laurie—why, they was practically in diapers. But after he won that old mares' race he took the kids into a fancy Western store and spent two hundred dollars outfitting them and never thought a thing of it, 'cause he had won that race, and old Mr. Doyle had made him all those promises, and— Well, he was *going* somewhere.

"I learned since that the years are hard on cowboys. Not having your own place, being someone else's foreman, running someone else's cattle—that's second-best, isn't it? Least, to Henry it is. Henry's not really been happy, here or anywhere, since Mr. Doyle died. Not till he tried to quit last month and Lester offered him this deal. Course, Lester owed him that, but, even so, it's better now, with Henry so hopeful. The other night, he called his mother, and he sounded so proud and happy—he said, 'Listen, Mama, I

132

own some cattle.' But, you know, it grieved me some, proud as he was, 'cause it could've been fifteen years ago and him calling his mama about those heifers of Mr. Doyle's. I guess that's what it's all about for a cowboy. Cows and calves and your own place and being free. Being up on a horse—being good at it, doing what you know best. Course, cowboying's changed so much with all them yearlings coming in. That's been some of what's bothering Henry—I mean, it's not been like he expected. Sometimes he says that working those yearlings is like being in a factory, only outdoors. I remember how we used to go to those Westerns, and there'd be this cowboy, looking so natural and realistic, like he just walked off some pasture into being a movie star. And this cowboy—things like money didn't mean a thing to him. I mean, I don't think Henry ever really expected to be fretting about money.

"Last fall, with my operation and Pearl and Laurie starting college, and then there was Henry needing his teeth fixed—why, we was so broke last fall we tore up our credit cards, and if you're from a ranch they won't let you cash a check in town without two credit cards to show with your driver's license. But Henry never would ask Lester about the money owing to him. It's just a hard thing to do, asking for money, if you're a cowboy. Especially with Lester. Lester is a real big guy for talking, but he's condescending. That's another thing that hurts Henry bad, 'cause there's no one supposed to be condescending to a cowboy. I guess we both should've known better. My granddaddy—my mother's daddy—he was a cowboy. Came to Texas by covered wagon and lived and died here. My daddy never really cowboyed. Once or twice, maybe, during the Depression, and after that he was always foreman in one of them big smelters. But he was one of eight and my mama was one of seven. I have so many cousins I can't name them all, and a lot of them cowboyed, and the rest, least in their hearts, was all hat-and-boot people. But growing up—they make ranch life so romantic when you're growing up. Like I said, we'd sit in those Westerns, and it looked so *right*, like something to be really proud of. I don't like Westerns anymore. There's some that's real filthy, and I wouldn't want my girls to go—not even Mattie, who's married. And the rest—well, I guess I've seen too much to be impressed. The movies I like now are the ones like 'Fiddler on the Roof' and 'The Sound of Music,' where love and kids are important, and a good Christian home. But Henry don't enjoy that sort of movie.

"It's not that he doesn't like his home. People say that cowboys—that if they wanted to be at home, they'd be at home. But it's not true. Cowboys *forget* about home. If Henry would call me when he's out and say where he was, I wouldn't worry. He's the most responsible man I know about his job, but not about me. He goes off alone, and it gets dark, and I say to myself, 'What if his jack fell and he's pinned under his pickup? What if his horse fell and he's out there freezing?' And I just sit. I don't like to call the neighbors, saying that he's not home. It hurts my pride, knowing they'll think he's in a bar or off on some stunt. That's one thing I can't understand—why a cowboy likes to be in bars. It's against my morals. If Henry left a bar early to come home to me, I'd be the happiest girl alive. We've had fights about that. I've screamed, locked him out, gone home to Mother, and nothing happens. And the funny thing is, I know Henry don't really *enjoy* drinking. I really believe Henry thinks it's wrong. I remember once we had a dance here, after a branding, and Henry went out and bought beer and bourbon for the men, and some of them got drunk and Henry was real ashamed afterward, 'cause the children saw it. Henry's really very moral. Cowboys are. They're conservative and Christian. I remember how shocked Henry was to find out the language Richard Nixon used. Henry was real disappointed in that.

"The first time I ever voted for a President, I voted for Kennedy. I'm not a Democrat, but I just couldn't bring myself to vote for Nixon, and Henry was real mad when I told him, 'cause he had heard that Kennedy, and his brother, too—that they went naked around the house. Henry said he wouldn't take me to vote. He said, 'You'll be the only Democrat, and everybody will know.' But the real reason was that he thought a politician should be moral, and it disgusted him, all those stories about Kennedy being naked. It was the same with Jimmy Carter. I kind of liked Jimmy Carter at first. Course, Henry didn't. He heard that Jimmy Carter was against welfare, and that was all right, 'cause we seen enough of that over in New Mexico—those poor Chicano women at home having all the children, and their men in bars, cashing their welfare checks for liquor. But Carter likes Negroes—least, that's what we heard—and Henry has this prejudice. All cowboys do, and it's something I don't understand, since they never really been around Negroes. Anyway, then there was this magazine deal, with Jimmy Carter talking about having adultery in his heart and lusting after women, and we were both shocked, hearing that. It sure made Henry's mind up real fast. I mean he'd never want a president who couldn't set no good example. Henry's real honorable. I remember once he and Tom and old Sam Otis—they were in town one night, and they pulled some stunt I don't even want to know about. Not that it was a real bad stunt. Henry says it was more a question of helping out this poor drunk woman with a problem. Well, there they were, helping this poor woman out, when the police came—two cars and three deputies—and I guess the police was kind of hard on old Sam, shoving him around, being really rough, and there's Sam just a poor, sick old cowpuncher. So Henry stepped in. He said something like 'Don't you think this fellow's kind of old?' and then I guess he must've started hitting, 'cause the police put handcuffs on him and he spent the night in jail. Anyhow, the next night at supper he was telling the girls about it. I said to him, 'Henry, aren't you ashamed to be telling this in front of the children? Wouldn't it embarrass *you*, hearing that *your* daddy spent a night in jail?' And Henry said no, it wouldn't—not if he knew his daddy had been taking up for someone. Well, that's the kind of cowboy Henry is. He's a good man—and all the drinking and the stunts, that's because of his disappointment. He sees me going to work, so tired all the time, and he knows it's to help him out, and he gets ashamed. I mean, he knows if we didn't need the money I'd be free for driving Melinda to her track meets or cheerleading practice. So he takes that bottle of bourbon from the chuck wagon. I used to empty those bottles fast as I found them, but I gave it up. I figure he's better off at the wagon than most places, and there's no point talking, 'cause that's not the sort of thing he'd feel comfortable talking to me about."

136

Betsy stopped for a long while, thinking. "You know," she said finally, "the other night we was sitting out behind the barn watching the sun set, and I don't recall as I've ever seen Henry so contented as he was right then, with just me and a glass of sweet iced tea for company."

Chapter 12

HENRY lost his deal with Lester Hill on a day in June when summer seemed to settle over the Panhandle like a cloak of heat. The grass was curing. The rich spring green of the pastures had begun to fade to the dry dull green of a tough scrub that would keep the cattle working for their nourishment through summer, and by early afternoon that day even the yearlings were sluggish, as if the morning's grazing had taken all the effort they could muster. They moved to their watering tanks with a kind of torpor. Nothing else moved at all. The horses rested under the cottonwoods and hackberries in the little grove by Henry's house. Melinda's cat slept in the middle of the courtyard. And out behind the barn a long, fat rattlesnake was sunning, coiled motionless on the trampled ground inside the cattle chute.

Henry had spent the morning with Calvin Pratt and Ed Loomis and three cowboys from the Triple R, mending half a mile of their joint fence, and then he had left them for the barn, to work on a broken blade from a windmill in one of the big ten-section cow pastures. Sam Otis was waiting at the barn to help him. Sam was sick again. He seemed to have shrivelled over the past month. His red, bourbon nose and pointy ears were suddenly enormous on his wasted face. His hands were like mitts at the end of his skinny arms, and his grizzled hair stuck up in dry patches on his head. Sam looked to Henry like some pitiful old clown dressed up in cowboy clothes. Tomorrow, he was going back into the hospital. He didn't want to go. He had fought against going. But the doctor had told Mabel Otis that without a lot of medicine and monitoring her husband would be dead in a month, and Mabel, who was as strong as she was bad-tempered, had promised to deliver him tomorrow morning if she had to rope him and drag him there. When Henry found out about the hospital, he sent for Sam, knowing that the old man would want to spend some time with his horse, Thunder, and would be too proud to come without the excuse of a day's work. Sam was good with windmills, actually. He and Henry had the blade mended in a few hours, and they were heading out in the pickup with it when Lester came in on the two-way radio.

Lester sounded so nervous that Henry and Sam grinned, hearing him at first, and made faces at the receiver.

"Hey, Henry," Lester said. "Henry, boy, I was just wondering. Henry, you remember those calves of mine? Nothing special, just those no-account Okies we run through the chute—you remember—back in April sometime."

Henry pushed the transmitter button. "What makes you think I'd be forgetting them?"

Sam looked out the window.

"Well, there's so many come and go," Lester said.

"They're doing real well," Henry said, and he nudged Sam. "You got to come out, take a look at them."

Lester started to talk about being busy with accounts lately. There was static, and it was difficult for Henry to hear.

"What's that?" Henry said finally.

Lester coughed and began again. His voice, on the radio, came and faded as the pickup bounced across the pasture toward the windmill. Henry was not in the habit of stopping his truck just to accommodate Lester Hill. He was barely even listening by the time Lester broke off his monologue and announced suddenly that he wanted his calves rounded up tomorrow. It looked like a droughty summer, Lester said, and he had had this offer for the calves. Not that he would make anything on them—just enough to cover his costs. And, of course, Henry would understand that he couldn't risk losing money on a droughty summer, not with a bank loan due and . . . Lester laughed, nervous. He had not once mentioned those calves to Henry—not since that day in the Buick when they made their deal. Henry had not expected him to mention them. Once a deal was made, there was no point in talking about it all the time.

"Tomorrow," Lester repeated.

Henry braked so fast that Sam nearly went through the

windshield. He grabbed the microphone. "We was grazing those calves for the feedyard! We got near two thousand calves dropped this spring. How about *them?* You ain't worried none about them being thirsty."

There was no reply. Henry mashed the button to say something, and thought better of it.

"Just have them gathered tomorrow. Tomorrow. Hear? I got trucks coming Friday morning." And then, soothing, "Course, I'd come by myself and take care of them if I weren't so damn busy. You know how it is, Henry, running a spread like this. The responsibilities."

Henry sat staring out the window.

"I sure do appreciate your taking care of this." Lester's voice was getting weaker. "I mean, I wouldn't want you going to no trouble with them calves. Not on my account. But, hell, friends is friends—right? And I know you'd—"

Henry switched off the radio. He was in a daze. He reached for his bottle, and then, without a word to Sam, he backed the truck around and started driving. It was four in the afternoon when he left the ranch for the highway, and it was after ten that night when Betsy, in the kitchen, heard the truck lurch into the courtyard. Henry and Sam sat there waiting, too drunk to move.

Betsy ran out of the kitchen door. She was frantic with worry. "Where you been, Henry? Henry! Sam!" She held a flashlight to the truck window. "Why, shame on you, Sam. You ought to be home in bed. You ought to be resting up for the hospital."

"I ain't going," Sam said.

Betsy opened the door and saw the empty bottles on the floor. "Oh, Sam," she said softly.

"Ain't nobody going to get me to that hospital."

"Come on, now, Sam, you know you don't mean that." Betsy reached up for Sam's knobby hand. Sam started down, trembling, and then he fell against her. She braced him with her shoulder and started to walk him slowly toward the house. "I just know you don't mean that," she said again.

"It's the truth, Betsy," Sam said. "When you're drunk, there's truth in you. It's when you're sober you're a politician, always saying what other folks want."

"Mabel's been calling," Betsy told him. "She's all set up. She's been carrying on, screaming at me real bad. She says she knows you and Henry was in some bar, and it's all Henry's fault, getting you drunk when you're—"

"Poor old Henry," Sam said, and he belched. "Everybody hates old Henry, 'cause he's always trying to help his friends out."

Betsy winced. "Where you been, Sam?"

"Well, Henry and me, we was driving along. We both been drinking a little. That is, *I* was drunk. Henry—he was sober. Anyhow, we found this old gal passed out on the road."

Betsy sighed.

"Now, Betsy, you wouldn't of even noticed her. Even me, at my age—I weren't interested. But you know how Henry is. He's a sure-enough gentleman. He said, 'We got to get this poor little lady out of here,' and so we just had a little drink on that and . . .'"

Betsy left Sam at the kitchen table and went back out to Henry. Henry's head was on the steering wheel. He was singing to himself.

142

"It weren't that at all, Betsy," Henry said when Betsy had pulled him out of the truck and was trying to move him across the courtyard. He leaned, heavy, on her shoulder, and she nearly fell. "It was just that old Sam—listen, Betsy, we was driving around with this here piece of windmill, and old Sam says, 'If I'm a-gonna die tomorrow, today I want to go to one of them places where indecent people are.' "

Even Betsy smiled.

"It's funny," Henry said. "Old people are like that. Here's Sam—he's had to work from the day he was old enough to do anything, and he's still working. Least, he thinks so. And, shoot, it's hard to get a wife to understand, but you can't leave old Sam on a day like today, even if you get in trouble. You can't say, 'Now, Sam, don't do that,' if it's something he wants to do, and what old Sam wants real bad is to be going back. Back to the good days, I mean. Every day like that just tickles him, and if he can get a young man like me to go back with him—why, it just means so much to that old cowpuncher." Henry stopped just short of the kitchen door and vomited. Betsy held his head.

"O.K.?" Betsy said.

Henry leaned against the house. "I guess this is the other part of cowboying, ain't it? The part when all the craziness comes out."

Just then, Sam started crying in the kitchen. Betsy ran in, with Henry stumbling behind her. "My gun, where's my gun," Sam was sobbing. "Now, why didn't I use that gun this morning? What do I got to live for?"

"You got me, Tom, Calvin," Henry began, and collapsed into a kitchen chair.

Betsy glared at him. "You got your wife, your children,

143

your grandchildren," she told Sam. "You got everything you did."

"I can't ride a bronc or rope a calf. I can't do it anymore."

"But you can enjoy seeing those grandkids of yours doing it," Betsy said.

Sam wiped his eyes, under thick, black-rimmed glasses. "It ain't the same seeing anyone else do it as doing it yourself. I used to ride out smooth on that bronc. I used to wave my hat. I can't do that anymore."

Betsy set a pot of coffee on the stove.

"Course, that grandson of mine, old Will—course he's not so good a cowpuncher as me, but he ain't bad, neither." Sam was warming. "I swear, last week I took that old bank of mine—I took my knife and cut that old bank right in half, and I bought that boy a four-hundred-dollar horse. Hell, he's a cowpuncher, that's the reason. You know what a cowpuncher is, Betsy—it's when you can ride in that pasture all day long, like old Will, and never say, 'Granddad, I'm thirsty. I want a glass of water, Granddad. I'm hungry.' "

"I'll tell you what a cowpuncher is," Henry cut in. "It ain't roping and it ain't riding bronc and it ain't being smart, neither. It's thinking enough about a dumb animal to go out in the rain or snow and try to save that cow. Not for the guy that owns the cow but for that poor old cow and her calf. It's getting down in that bog—in quicksand, if you got the guts. You tie up one leg, then the other. You tramp her out. You get her laying on her side and then you get your horse and you drag that old cow out of the quicksand."

Sam nodded, groggy.

144

"You see, Betsy, this old cow, she don't know but what you're trying to kill her. But you drag her out, even if she's fighting you, and then you ride a mile yonder and find another danged old cow bogged down the same way."

Sam chuckled while tears ran down his bony cheeks.

"Now, Sam, who's going to teach little Will all those things unless you're there to teach him?" Betsy said gently.

"I am," Sam said.

"You see, you got something to live for," Betsy told him.

Melinda passed through the kitchen on her way to bed. She had stayed up late in the parlor, watching "Planet of the Apes" on television, but her hair was already set and she had got her homework and her Bible reading out of the way right after supper. "Well, hello there, Sam," she said brightly before she disappeared.

Sam hardly heard her. He was busy now arranging objects on the kitchen table. He had taken a package of Kents, a bottle of Vitamin C, and a book—it was "Secrets of the Heart," Betsy's new Gibran—from the revolving tray, and, explaining that the book was a gate, the cigarettes were a cow, and the vitamins a cowboy, he was showing Betsy his special method for luring cows into pens. "You got to have patience till she sees the gate," he said, moving the vitamins cautiously behind the cigarettes. "If you run her hard, you got to rope her and drag her through that gate, and then the next time she sees a cowpuncher she's going to turn and run and go wild. Now, you know well as I do there's no one going to make money off a wild cow."

"Have some coffee, Sam," Betsy said.

"And there's another thing that's good, if it's a wild steer. You can tie that old steer to a tree, and then you take a

145

burro and feed it oats, and *then* you let that old steer get real tired, walking around the tree all night, and, course, the burro gets hungry on its own—you know how them burros do like oats—and then when the steer's real tired and the burro's real hungry, you tie the steer to the burro and the burro'll bring him right in to where he got those oats before." Sam took a long breath. "Course, that's a little complicated, but I did bring in fifty of them outlaw steer that way once." Sam was cheering up now. He told Betsy that he had another story for her. "This is such a gosh-darn good story, Betsy, that you won't believe it."

"Yeah, I will."

"Bet you don't." Sam was delighted. Neither of them had noticed Henry wander off into the parlor. He was sitting there, on Betsy's wild-flower couch, staring at the blank television screen.

"It's about the day I got that crazy steer I'd been after near two years," Sam said. "I brought him in with my hotshot. I took that old hotshot to the blacksmith and he put tin on the barrel—put in new batteries, too. Boy, them batteries was so strong—why, when I tried that hotshot out on the one-eyed wetback at the gas station he jumped ten feet and howled." Sam banged the table, laughing. "That old wetback said, 'You know, Mr. Sam, I thought for a minute the vision had come back in that bad eye of mine.'"

Just then, the phone rang. Henry ran in for it. He was thinking of Lester, thinking that maybe Lester had reconsidered, changed his mind. When he heard Mabel Otis howling at him, he handed the phone to Betsy without a word. He signalled to Sam, and the two of them tried to tiptoe from the house. Betsy, on the phone, was calming

146

Mabel, saying that the boys were just enjoying a cup of coffee. No, the boys had already left, and there was the truck—could Mabel hear it?—starting. Henry was driving Sam home.

Henry spent the night in his pickup. He delivered Sam, but he did not have the heart to face Betsy with the news that his deal with Lester was over. He did not know what to do, and so he parked on the cowpath, out of sight, and tried to sleep off his despair. The dawn woke him—the weak pink light of another hot day pushing at the clearer darkness. He reached for a bottle, found it empty, and lit a cigarette instead. The taste in his mouth was foul. His head was pounding. A kind of helpless fury came over him as he sat smoking, and made his hand shake. He ground out the cigarette and jumped down from the truck. There was something black moving toward him down the cowpath. He squinted into the hazy morning light, trying to focus. It was a bull on the path. Not a Willow bull—they were safely fenced in a back pasture—but one of the huge Brangus from the Triple R. Behind it was another bull, and then another. Three bulls in all—a line of black studs stalking Henry's pasture. Henry swore to himself and ran for the pickup. He drove to the house as fast as the truck would go. There was a light in the kitchen, and Henry knew from the light that Betsy had been waiting up all night for him, but he did not stop. He opened the barn, saddled Pepper, and backed the pickup to the horse trailer. Twenty minutes later, he was banging on the door of Ed Loomis's camper, seven miles from headquarters, shouting for him to wake up and get his horse.

It took a while for Henry and Ed to round the bulls up.

The bulls had disappeared from the cowpath, and the men rode the pasture, searching, until they came to a heifer sprawled flat and frothing—and so worked over she could not get up. After that, they found the bulls easily. There was a moment, with the bulls shut in the corral at Ed's camp, when Henry thought of calling the foreman at the Triple R to come and claim them, to settle up, man to man, for the wasted cow. The moment passed. Henry flipped the circle of rope in his hand until it felt just right to him, and then he opened the corral gate. He worked hard for his first bull. Ed was too excited to be much help roping, and Henry had to tie his rope to his horse to hold the bull once they finally had him down.

Henry took his knife out. "The way I see it, it's like you had a daughter and she was raped," he said, and then he cut.

For a minute, he felt better. By the time he had roped and thrown the next bull, he knew that he was not expressing right—not expressing right at all—but by then there was nothing he could do about it.